# HOW TO BE
# MASSIVE

YOU SAID I COULD DO WHATEVER I WANTED IN LIFE ONCE I PUT MY MIND TO IT, SO I DID.

IN LOVING MEMORY OF GRAINNE DOOLEY.

# HOW TO BE
# MASSIVE

WRITTEN AND ILLUSTRATED BY
AOIFE DOOLEY

GILL BOOKS

GILL BOOKS
HUME AVENUE
PARK WEST
DUBLIN 12
WWW.GILLBOOKS.IE

GILL BOOKS IS AN IMPRINT OF M.H. GILL & CO.

© AOIFE DOOLEY 2016

978 0717I 7270 2

PRINTED BY BZ GRAF, POLAND

THE PAPER USED IN THIS BOOK
COMES FROM THE WOOD PULP OF
MANAGED FORESTS. FOR EVERY
TREE FELLED, AT LEAST ONE TREE
IS PLANTED, THEREBY RENEWING
NATURAL RESOURCES.

A CIP CATALOGUE
RECORD FOR THIS BOOK
IS AVAILABLE FROM THE
BRITISH LIBRARY.

5 4 3 2 1

# CONTENTS

HEYA! ME NAME'S NIKITA AND I'M 22 YEARS YOUNG, BORN AND BRED IN COOLOCK, DUBLIN. I LIVE WITH ME MA, DA, POX OF A BROTHER JAYO AND ME LIL' DOGGY TIESTO. I LOVE ME FELLA ANTO. STOP! WOULD BE LOST WITHOUT HIM, HE'S ME WORLD. AND, OF COURSE, ME BESTO TANYA, SHE'S ALWAYS UP FOR HAVIN' THE BANTS.

ANYWAYS, ME NERVES ARE GOIN' POXY 90! CAN'T BELIEVE I'M AFTER WRITIN' ME FIRST BOOK! I'D LIKE TO THANK THE ACADEMY AND ALL ME FANS FOR TAKIN' THE TIME TO STALK ME PAGE ON A DAILY BASIS. YIZ ARE BANG ON! SOUND OUT! AND TO ALL ME HATERS – KEEP ON HATIN' YIZ ROTTEN TICKS. NOT MY FAULT I WAS BORN MASSIVE, CAME STRAIGH' OUT OF THE ROTUNDA LIKE THIS.

# HOW TO MAKE YOUR HAIR MASSIVE

THE FIRST STEP TO BEIN' MASSIVE IS HAVIN' MASSO HAIR. YOUR HAIR IS THE FIRST THING THA' SOMEONE NOTICES ABOUT YE, EVEN BEFORE YIZZER TEETH! SO IF YE HAVEN'T GOT ANY TEETH AND YOU'RE A GUMMY POX DON'T BE WORRYIN' ABOUT IT, RIGH'. I'LL BE SHOWIN' YE WHAT PRODUCTS TO USE TO MAKE YIZZER HAIR AS STUNNIN' AS CAN BE AND, OF COURSE, ME SIGNATURE HAIRSTYLE THE 'HUN BUN', ALONG WITH OTHER BITS AND PIECES, YEAH.

# WHA' IS A HUN BUN?

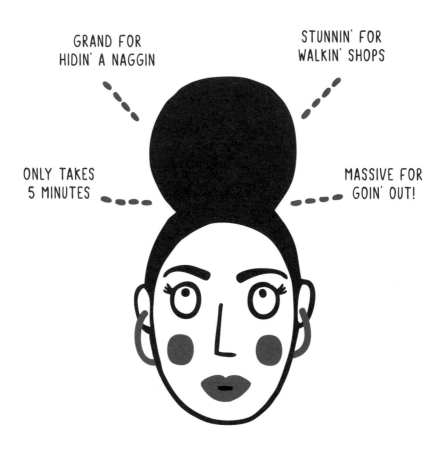

GRAND FOR
HIDIN' A NAGGIN

STUNNIN' FOR
WALKIN' SHOPS

ONLY TAKES
5 MINUTES

MASSIVE FOR
GOIN' OUT!

THIS IS ME FAVOURITE HAIRSTYLE IN THE ACTUAL WORLD. SWEAR DOWN, I WEAR ME HAIR LIKE THIS ALL THE TIME - WHEN I'M GOIN' SHOPS AND WHEN I'M GOIN' ON A NIGH' OUT WITH THE GIRLS. YOUR ONE SAOIRSE RONAN WORE ONE ON THE RED CARPET AN' ALL AND SHE LOOKED BLEEDIN' MASSIVE. IF YE WANT YIZZER HAIR TO LOOK STUNNIN' 24-7 THEN THIS IS THE HAIRSTYLE FOR YOU, HUN.

# HOW TO DO A HUN BUN
## -IN FOUR PURE EASY STEPS-

REEF YIZZER HAIR UP IN A HIGH PONY. IF YE HAVE NO HAIR THEN IT'S GRAND, JUST CLIP IN SOME EXTENSIONS, HUN.

SPRAY SOME HAIRSPRAY IN SO YE CAN GET IT MAD BIG - THE BIGGER THE BUN, THE BIGGER THE HUN.

TWIST IT AROUND THE BOBBIN ALL THE WAY UNTIL YE MEET THE TIP OF YIZZER HAIR.

CHECK HOW MASSIVE YE ARE BY POSTIN' A PIC ON FACEBOOK. IF YE GET MORE THAN 30 LIKES THEN YOU'RE MASSIVE.

# WHA' TO HIDE IN YOUR HUN BUN

STICK A NAGGIN IN YIZZER BUN WHEN YOU'RE GOIN' OUT. THE BOUNCERS NEVER CATCH YE, SWEAR ON ME NANNY'S GRAVE. I DO IT ALL THE TIME.

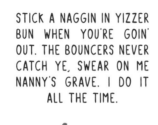

HIDE A EURDO IN YOUR BUN. IT'S LIKE WHEN YE FIND A FIVER IN YOUR POCKET DOIN' THE WASHIN', CHUFFED!

EMERGENCY SMOKES

THE BUTTONS OFF THE TELLY SO YOUR POX OF A FELLA CAN'T WATCH THE FOOTBALL.

LIPSTICK, SO IF SOME POX ASKS YE FOR A LEND OF SOME YE CAN SAY YE HAVE NONE.

# HAIR TYPES

BEFORE I GO ON TO GIVE YE ANY MORE TIPS, WHY DON'T YE HAVE
A LOOK AND SEE WHA' TYPE OF HAIR YE HAVE? NOW, IF YOUR HAIR
IS ROTTEN DON'T START SOBBIN', COS NIKITA IS HERE TO FIX YE
RIGH' UP! SO WIPE THEM TEARS AND CHIN UP, HUN.

| | | | |
|---|---|---|---|
| WAVY | CURLY | CRIMPED | STRAIGH' |
| YOUR HAIR IS DEAD, HUN | PURE TICK | KNOTTY POX | FELLA'S PUBE |
| GREASY AN' ALL | KINKY | STRUCK BY LIGHTNIN' | FANNY STUBBLE |

# WHEN YOUR HAIR IS A LOAD OF POX

NOT ALL OF US ARE LUCKY ENOUGH TO BE BORN MASSIVE, BUT I WAS ONE OF THE LUCKY ONES. I CAME STRAIGH' OUT OF THE ROTUNDA LOOKIN' THIS GOOD. IF YOUR HAIR IS A LOAD OF POX, USE THESE TWO THINGS. SWEAR! THEY WORK WONDERS FOR ME HAIR TO ADD A BIT OF VOLUME, YE KNOW? AFTER YE USE THESE, ADD A BIT OF HAIR SPRAY TO KEEP IT IN PLACE SO IT DOESN'T BLOW ALL OVER THE GAFF.

# MAKE A STATEMENT

THIS IS A PIC OF ME LAST NIGH' IN WRIGHTS. SWEAR! DIDN'T LOOK
LIKE THIS THE NEXT MORNIN' - WAS POXY DYIN'. SOMETIMES WHEN
ME HAIR JUST ISN'T GOIN' THE WAY I WANT IT, I COVER THE PARTS
THA' ARE STICKIN' OUT WITH SOMETHIN', LIKE THIS BINDI HEADBAND.
IT JUST GIVES YIZZER BUN A LITTLE MORE SPARKLE AND IT'S GREAT
FOR CATCHIN' A FELLA'S EYE IN THE CLUB.

# HAIRSTYLES AND TRENDS

THESE ARE SOME HAIRSTYLES AND TRENDS YE DO SEE AROUND TOWN. SOME OF THEM ARE ROTTEN BUT I CAN'T SAY ANYTHIN' COS I'VE HAD A FEW OF THEM MESELF. SCARLEH FOR ME AND TANYA IN SCHOOL WITH OUR SPICER MULLETS. WE THOUGHT WE WERE BLEEDIN' MASSIVE AND THE HACK OF US. SOMETIMES YE LOSE THE TOUCH BUT IF YE WERE BORN MASSIVE IT ALWAYS COMES BACK TO YE.

THE 'HIGH PONY'

THE 'FANNY SPLIT'

THE 'SPICER MULLET'

THE 'STRAIGHTENED FOR 5 HOURS'

THE 'FESTIVAL HUN BUNS'

THE 'I'M VEGAN, DID I TELL YE THA' ALREADY?'

THE 'JEDWARD'

THE 'HUN BUN'

THE 'IRISH DANCIN' WIG'

THE 'LET ME TALK
TO THE MANAGER'

THE 'SIDE FANNY
SPLIT ALTAR BOY'

THE 'MUNNER FRINGE'

THE 'I'VE RUINED
ME POXY HAIR'

THE 'LICK ARSE'

THE 'SHANTAY
YOU STAY HUN'

# MASSO HAIR ACCESSORIES

THESE ARE THE TOP HAIR ACCESSORIES EVERY HUN SHOULD HAVE IN THEIR GAFF TO KEEP THEIR HAIR LOOKIN' MASSIVE ALL YEAR ROUND. SWEAR DOWN! THA' FLOWER HEADBAND IS STUNNIN' - REMINDS ME OF WHEN I WENT TO SEE AVICII WITH THE GIRLS! AWH STOP! GAGGIN' FOR THE SUMMER, XOX.

DOUGHNUT FOR MAKIN' YIZZER BUN BIGGER

A HAIR DRYER, OBVIOUSLY LIKE

A BINDI HAIRBAND - PURE MASSIVE!

A FESTIVAL FLOWER HEADBAND

BOBBINS FOR PUTTIN' YIZZER
HAIR IN A BUN

BOBBY PINS - USUALLY FOUND
ON THE FLOOR

ONE OF THEM HAIRBANDS THA'
YE GET IN PENNEYS

GHD FOR MAKIN' YIZZER HAIR
MAD STRAIGH' AN' ALL

A BRUSH THA' ISN'T FULL OF
YOUR SISTER'S POXY HAIR

A COMB FOR MAKIN' YIZZER
HAIR BIG

# NIKITA'S
## TOP ACCESSORIES, XOX

THESE ARE ME TOP HAIR ACCESSORIES THA' I USE ALL THE TIME.
I NEVER LEAVE THE GAFF WITHOUT ME EXTENSIONS OR CLIP-IN BUN.
ROLLERS ARE VERDY GOOD FOR KEEPIN' YIZZER HAIR VOLUMISED WHEN
IT LOOKS ROTTEN. ALWAYS HAVE A CLIP FOR SAFETY SO WHEN YOU'RE
RUNNIN' FOR THE BUS YE DON'T HAVE TO WORRY ABOUT LOSIN' YOUR
EXTENSIONS, RIGH'.

HAIR EXTENSIONS, SWEAR! ME
NO.1 ACCESSORY.

ROLLERS FOR GIVIN' YIZZER FLAT
HAIR SOME MASSIVENESS.

CLAW CLIP FOR KEEPIN' YIZZER
BUN FROM BLOWIN' ALL OVER
THE GAFF.

CLIP-IN STUN HUN BUN FOR
BALDY POXES.

# WHA' TO SAY TO A HAIRDRESSER
## WHEN THEY ASK WHA' YE DID AT THE WEEKEND

## MONTH YE WERE BORN

JAN I WENT TO THE SHOPS AND
FEB I LISTENED TO ADELE AND
MAR WENT TO BENIDORM AND
APR WAS IN A ROTTEN MOOD SO
MAY DIDN'T DO MUCH, JUST
JUN AWH STOP HUN, I

JUL I WENT ON A MAD ONE AND I
AUG WAS DYING AND
SEP I HAD A SMOKE AND
OCT SWEAR! GAS WEEKEND,
NOV NOTHING MUCH, JUST
DEC WAS IN A HOOP AND

## FIRST LETTER OF YIZZER NAME

A GOT A BACKER OFF TUPAC TO TESCO
B GAVE ME NANNY A JOCKEYBACK TO MASS
C LICKED PHIL MITCHELL'S BALDY HEAD
D ATE A SIX PACK OF MEANIES IN THE NIP
E WENT TO PENNEYS WITH BEYONCÉ
F DRANK A NAGGIN WITH JUSTIN BIEBER
G ATE A HAM SAMBO WITH RAMBO
H WATCHED THE ANGELUS WITH DRAKE
I SEEN THE ROCK GET A PEDI
J BALLED WATCHING EASTENDERS
K WENT TO MASS WITH MILEY CYRUS
L WENT TO SIN WITH ME GRANDA, HE'S GAS
M WENT ON A MAD ONE WITH BRESSIE

N WENT TO THE ILAC WITH KIMMY K
O WENT TO THE PICTURES WITH MEL GIBBO
P WENT TO THE PLEX WITH BILL MURRAY
Q WENT TO MCDONALD'S WITH OPRAH
R GOT SICK IN TOM CRUISE'S AIR MAX
S WENT TO THE BLACKER WITH YOUR MA
T MET ICE-T FOR A BIT OF LUNCH
U ATE A PIECE OF BILLY ROLL ON THE BUS
V HAD A BOWL OF CODDLE WITH ICE CUBE
W BOUGHT A CHICKEN FILLET ROLL
X LOST ME EXTENSIONS IN THE LIFFEY
Y WAS SOBBING AT FAIR CITY, SWEAR!
Z GOT A SPICEBAG WITH JEZZA KYLE

# HOW TO MAKE SURE YIZZER MAKE-UP IS ON POINT

GRAND! NOW THA' YE HAVE YIZZER HAIR SORTED, LET'S MOVE ON TO YOUR MAKE-UP TO MAKE SURE IT'S ON POINT. I LOVE NOTHIN' MORE THAN DOIN' ME MAKE-UP, BUT SWEAR, SOMETIMES IT JUST DOESN'T GO THE WAY I WANT IT, AND WE ALL KNOW HOW THAT ENDS UP: 'I'M NOT GOIN' OUT'. I'LL SHOW YIZ EVERYTHIN': HOW TO CONTOUR YOUR FACE, GETTIN' YOUR EYEBROWS ON FLEEK, THE DIFFERENCE BETWEEN INSTAGRAM AND REAL LIFE, COS LET'S FACE IT, NO ONE'S POXY PERFECT! MOST THINGS ARE AIR-BRUSHED THESE DAYS, EVEN CHICKEN FILLET ROLLS IN MAGAZINES!

# HOW TO BE A MUA

- PUT 'MUA' AFTER YIZZER NAME ON FACEBOOK SO PEOPLE KNOW YOU'RE A PRO ✔

- MAKE A BLOG SO YE CAN SHOW EVERYONE HOW YE CAN MAKE PEOPLE LOOK MASSO ✔

- DO A DAY MAKE-UP COURSE ✔

♡ ⅲⅲ

HERE'S A STEP-BY-STEP LIST YE CAN GO BY TO SEE IF YE ARE A MUA HUN. IT'S IMPORTANT TO HAVE GOOD FRIENDS, BUT IT'S EVEN MORE IMPORTANT TO HAVE FRIENDS WHO CAN MAKE YE LOOK MASSIVE ON A DAILY BASIS. STOP! WOULD BE LOST WITHOUT MY TANYA DOIN' ME HAIR AND MAKE-UP FOR ME, SHE'S VERDY GOOD.

# HOW TO CONTOUR
# YIZZER FACE

FOR GIVIN' YE THA'
HOLLYWOOD NOSE JOB
YE ALWAYS WANTED

FOR GIVIN' YIZZER
FIVEHEAD A LIFT

FOR GIVIN' YE
BONE STRUCTURE

FOR GETTIN' RID
OF THE CHINS YE
DON'T WANT IN
YIZZER LIFE

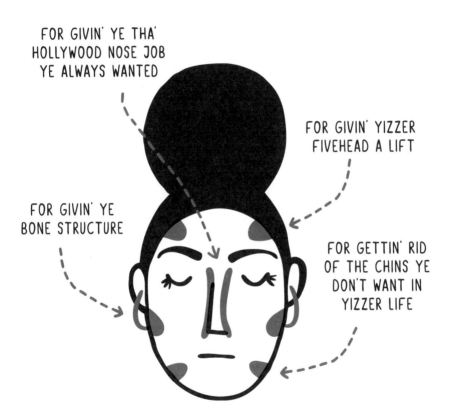

IF YE EAT 5 SPICEBAGS A WEEK LIKE ME, CONTOURIN' IS A GREAT
WAY FOR HIDIN' YIZZER DOUBLE CHINS. IT'S USUALLY BETTER
THOUGH IF YE HAVE ONE OF YOUR MUA HUNS DO IT FOR YE COS
IT'S HARDER THAN IT LOOKS. STOP! YE WANNA SEE ME THE FIRST
TIME I DONE IT! I GAVE MESELF 4 POXY CHINS WHEN I WAS
SUPPOSED TO GET RID OF THE 2 I ALREADY HAD.

# EYEBROWS ON FLEEK
## (YE TICK)

THE 'STUN HUN'

THE 'YOU FOR POXY REAL?'

THE 'TOO MAD'

THE 'SEE YOU, YE TICK'

THE 'BLIND BOY'

THE 'NIKE TICK'

THE 'YOU STARTIN'?'

THE 'TADPOLE'

THE 'UNIBROW'

THE 'I'M SNAPPIN'

THE 'ADIDAS SLITS'

THE 'DRAG QUEEN'

THE 'CALM DOWN ON THE
EYEBROWS LUV'

THE 'AWH STOP,
THAT'S TERRIBLE HUN'

# INSTAGRAM VS. REAL LIFE

WE ALL HAVE THA' POX OF A FRIEND WHO IS CONSTANTLY
POSTIN' SELFIES. 'BAD PIC OF ME', THEY DO SAY. ME BOLLIX IT
IS! YE SPENT AN HOUR TAKIN' PICS FOR A NEW PROFILER! HERE'S
HOW YE CAN TELL IF THE PIC IS FILTERED TO BITS.

### INSTAGRAM

THE CLASSIC 'STUN HUN' FACE
POSE - MASSIVE!

### REAL LIFE

WHEN YE SEE THEM IN THE
CENTRA THE NEXT DAY

THE 'MASSO ARSE' POSE

THE PICS ON YOUR FRIEND'S PHONE
BEFORE THE INSTAGRAM FILTERS

# HOW TO TAKE A MASSIVE SELFIE

MASSIVE XOX

ADD IN AN INSPIRATIONAL QUOTE TO MAKE YIZZER SELFIE MEANINGFUL AN' ALL.

PICK YOUR POSE. I LOVE THE 'STUN HUN' - I DO IT ALL THE TIME IN ME PICS.

YE WANT TO GET YIZZER BODY IN TOO AND NOT JUST YIZZER HEAD.

HOLD THE PHONE LIKE THIS AND TAKE THE SELFIE WITH YIZZER THUMB.

# MAKE-UP NO-NOS

SWEAR! THESE ARE SOME MAKE-UP TRENDS YE DO SEE AROUND TOWN THA' WRECK ME HEAD. ALL THE YOUNG ONES LOOK THE POXY SAME! WILL YIZ CALM DOWN, YIZ ARE ONLY GOIN' TO THE CENTRA TO GET SOME MILK FOR YOUR MA, NOT THE BLEEDIN' VIP STYLE AWARDS. LESS IS MORE HUN, JUST SAYIN'.

LIP LINER ON TOP OF YIZZER LIPS. EVERYONE KNOWS THEY'RE NOT REAL, YE TICK!

EYEBROWS BIGGER THAN A GAFF ON THE SOUTHSIDE

A BINDI DIAMOND - ELECTRIC PICNIC ISN'T FOR ANOTHER 5 MONTHS, YE SAP

EYE SHADOW LIKE THIS, SWEAR! YIZ LOOK LIKE YE FELL INTO PAT BUTCHER'S MAKE-UP BAG

# THE STRUGGLE IS REAL

WE'VE ALL BEEN HERE, THERE'S NOTHIN' POXY WORSE.

WHEN YE CAN'T GET THE
STROKE THE EXACT SAME
ON THE OTHER SIDE!

WHEN YE SNEEZE AFTER
PUTTIN' ON YIZZER MASCARA

TAKIN' OFF EYELINER

WHEN THE EYELINER
JUST WON'T GO ON

WHEN YOU'RE SOBBIN' AND YOUR
WATERPROOF MASCARA ISN'T
POXY WATERPROOF

WHEN YOUR FELLA HAS BETTER
EYELASHES THAN YE

25

# TAN AN' ALL

YOUR TAN IS A VITAL PART OF BEIN' MASSIVE, SWEAR! EVEN THROUGH THE WINTER YE WANT TO KEEP THA' STUNNIN' GLOW AND YE WANT PEOPLE TO ASK YE, 'AH, WERE YE ON YOUR HOLLIERS?' THESE ARE SOME OF THE THINGS THA' WILL HELP YE NOT TO LOOK LIKE A PALE POX.

TAN WIPES FROM PENNEYS, GREAT FOR A NIGH' OUT

A TANNIN' MIT, COS NO ONE LIKES TO RUIN THEIR FLUFFY SOCKS

SPRAY-ON TAN IS THE BEST WAY TO GET YOUR STUNNIN' GLOW FOR THE SUMMER

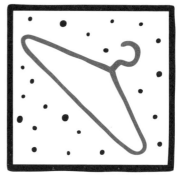

WHEN YE CAN'T REACH YIZZER BACK, PUT YOUR MIT ON AN OLD HANGER AND YOU'RE SORTED

# MAKE-UP ESSENTIALS

THESE ARE SOME OF ME ESSENTIALS I USE GETTIN' READY FOR A NIGH' OUT. YE CAN'T GO WRONG WITH A NAKED 2 PALLET. I LOVE ME DARK COLOURS AROUND THE EYES, MAKES YE LOOK MAD MYSTERIOUS OR SOMETHIN'. ME EYELASH CURLER WORKS WONDERS TOO COS I DON'T HAVE MAD LONG EYELASHES LIKE ME FELLA ANTO, THE POX!

LIPGLOSS

NAKED 2

# NIKITA'S
## COSMETICS

WHEN I WIN THE LOTTO AND I'M ALL OVER THE PAPERS AN' ALL, THAT'S WHEN I'M GONNA BRING OUT ME OWN MAKE-UP RANGE. STOP! THAT'S ME DREAM.

SPICEBAG LIPSTICK - THE SPICE MAKES YIZZER LIPS TINGLE AND LOOK BIGGER

2 IN 1 VODKA CLEANSER THA' YE CAN DRINK - GRAND FOR SNEAKIN' ON THE PLANE

FOR THA' GOLDEN GLOW YE CAN'T GET ANYWHERE ELSE, NIKITA HAS YIZ COVERED

EYELASH GLUE THA' DOESN'T SMELL LIKE A ROTTEN FANNY - NOTHIN' POXY WORSE!

# WHA' DO YOUR EYELASHES SAY ABOUT YOU?

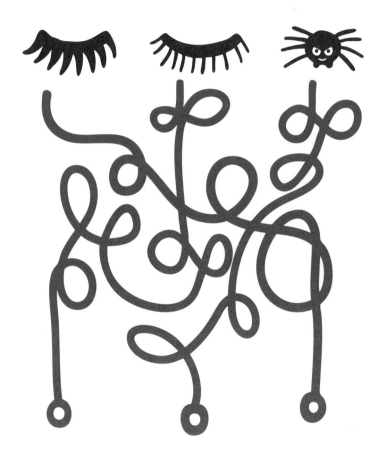

YOU'RE GOIN' A BIT BALDY BUT IT'S ALRIGH', HUN. JUST GET SOME FAKE ONES AND POP THEM ON AND YOU'RE BRAND NEW.

EH, THAT'S A POXY SPIDER, YE TICK! GET AWAY FROM ME WITH THA'.

YOUR EYELASH GAME IS ON POINT AND YOU KNOW IT, HUN. OWN THEM EYEBALL HAIRS AND HOLD YIZZER HEAD HIGH, TONIGH' IS YOUR NIGH'.

# THINGS EVERY STUN HUN SHOULD HAVE

THERE ARE CERTAIN THINGS THA' EVERY TRUE 'STUN HUN' SHOULD HAVE AND THIS SECTION GOES THROUGH EVERYTHING YE NEED, FROM PHONES AND APPS TO GEL NAILS, TATTOOS AND EVEN BODY ENHANCERS, RIGH'. I DON'T LEAVE THE GAFF WITHOUT HAVIN' ME PHONE IN ONE HAND AND ME LIGHTER IN THE OTHER. WHEN YOU'RE MASSIVE IT'S A DEVOTION TO STAY THIS STUNNIN', SO GET READY TO CHANGE YIZZER LIFESTYLES, YE TICKS.

# WHAT'S IN YOUR BAG?

ME BAG IS ME LIFE BUT IT'S USUALLY JUST FULL OF PENNEYS RECEIPTS, EMPTY MEANIES PACKETS AND STUFF THA' I'VE BEEN PRAYIN' FOR ST ANTHONY TO FIND THAT'S BEEN LOST FOR YEARS, AND IT'S ALWAYS SOMEWHERE DOWN THE END OF ME POXY BAG. WHEN I'M GETTIN' A NEW BAG I ALWAYS GO FOR A BLACK ONE COS THEY GO WITH EVERYTHIN'. I TRY TO GO FOR A SMALLER ONE TOO COS ME FELLA ANTO IS ALWAYS ASKIN' ME CAN I MIND HIS KEYS, CAN I MIND HIS MONEY, CAN I MIND THIS, CAN I MIND THA' - IT'S HEAD MELTIN'.

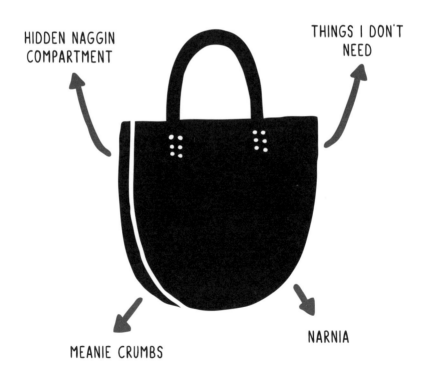

HIDDEN NAGGIN COMPARTMENT

THINGS I DON'T NEED

MEANIE CRUMBS

NARNIA

# BAG ESSENTIALS

THESE ARE SOME OF THE ESSENTIAL BITS AND PIECES
YIZ WILL FIND IN A HUN'S BAG AFTER A NIGH' OUT!

DEODORANT FOR
KEEPIN' YE PURE
FRESH THROUGHOUT
THE DAY

SENTIMENTAL LIGHTER
YOUR MA BROUGHT YE
BACK FROM IBIZA

TAMPON FOR OBVIOUS
REASONS AND GRAND
FOR SOAKIN' UP
VODKA SPILLS

LOOSE CHANGE SO YE
CAN GET A SPICEBAG
ON THE WAY HOME
FROM A NIGH' OUT

CHEWIN' GUM AND YOUR
PILL YE FORGOT TO
TAKE 3 DAYS AGO

RECEIPTS FOR FOOD,
DRINK AND SHOPPIN' IN
PENNEYS AN' ALL

# BODY BOOSTERS

THESE ARE ME TOP PRODUCTS FOR GIVIN' YIZZER BODY THE BOOST IT DESERVES WITHOUT HAVIN' TO LIFT A FINGER. SOME OF THEM ARE PURE ROTTEN BUT THEY WORK 110 PERCENT. SWEAR ON ME LIFE, NO JOKE. THE HOOP ENHANCER IS ME PERSONAL FAVOURITE AND LOOKS STUNNIN' WITH A BODYCON.

HOOP ENHANCER FOR GIVIN' YE A BIGGER HOOP

CHICKEN FILLETS FOR GIVIN' YE AN EXTRA CUP SIZE

THA' YOKE FOR YOUR LIPS TO MAKE THEM LOOK BIGGER – PERFECT FOR STUN HUN POSIN'

A FANNY PAD TO GIVE YE BIGGER HIPS – JUST STICK THEM ON YIZZER SIDE, NOT A BOTHER!

# JEWELLERY

MEDALLION
STATEMENT RINGS

A PURE GOLD CHAIN TO SHOW
THA' YOU'RE PURE CLASSY

HOOP EARRINGS THA' ARE
BIGGER THAN YIZZER HEAD

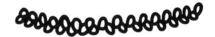

A BLACK CHOKER THA'
GOES WITH EVERYTHIN'

MAKE A STATEMENT WITH SOME STUNNIN' JEWELLERY ESSENTIALS. I DON'T LEAVE ME GAFF WITHOUT ME ENGAGEMENT RING ON. THA' POX ANTO PUT IT IN A SPICEBAG WHEN HE WAS GOIN' TO PROPOSE AND I SWALLYED IT. WAS IN THE POXY HOSTIPAL FOR AGES WAITIN' FOR IT TO COME OUT. ANYWAYS, A NICE PAIR OF EARRINGS OR A STATEMENT CHOKER DOES THE JOB FOR ME ON A NIGH' OUT.

# -NAILS BY NIKITA-

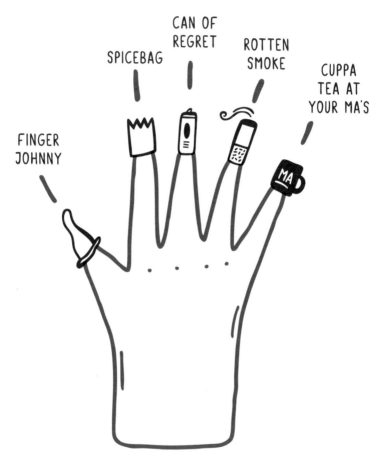

FINGER JOHNNY

SPICEBAG

CAN OF REGRET

ROTTEN SMOKE

CUPPA TEA AT YOUR MA'S

AWH STOP! I LOVE GETTIN' ME NAILS DONE, ESPECIALLY WHEN YOU'RE GOIN' ON YIZZER HOLLIERS. YE JUST FEEL MAD FRESH OR SOMETHIN', THERE'S NOTHIN' BETTER. ONLY GOT MINE DONE YESTERDAY - THEY'RE MASSIVE. WHEN YOU'RE GETTIN' YIZZER NAILS DONE YE SHOULD GO ALL OUT AND GET SOMETHIN' STUNNIN'. THESE ARE SOME OF ME FAVOURITES ON THE NEXT PAGE.

HOLY GOD NAIL

LOVEHEART TIP

HAIRY HOOP NAIL

LEOPARD PRINT
NAIL

DIAMONDS ARE A
HUN'S BEST FRIEND

STRIPED NAIL

KISSIN' EMOJI
NAIL

AZTEC HOLLIERS
NAIL

SPOOKY GHOST
POX NAIL

NAGGIN NAIL

SPOTTY
POX NAIL

RELATIONSHIP
STATUS NAIL

POKE YIZZER
EYE OUT NAIL

I SEE POXY
EVERYTHIN' NAIL

BLUNT NAIL

PINT OF
GUINNESS NAIL

# TATTOO TYPES

NOTHIN' SAYS 'FAMILY' MORE THAN GETTIN' A TATTOO FOR A LOVED ONE ON YIZZER BODY. STOP! I HAVE ANTO'S NAME ON ME, BUT THAT'S ONLY COS WE'RE ENGAGED NOW, AND IF I SEE SOME POX FLIRTIN' WITH HIM I SHOW THEM ME TATTOO AND THEY JOG ON.

STARS FOR EACH
OF YOUR KIDDIES

YOUR FELLA'S NAME SO
EVERYONE KNOWS HE'S
YOURS AN' ALL

ROSARY BEADS TO KEEP
YIZZER CANKLE BLESSED

CLASSIC TRAMP STAMP, LOOKS MASSO
WITH A BIKINI ON YIZZER HOLLIERS

# PIERCINGS

I LOVE ME PIERCINGS. I REMEMBER ME AND TANYA GOIN' UP TO NORTHSIDE SHOPPIN' CENTRE TO GET OUR BELLIES DONE. SHE WAITED AROUND THE CORNER AND PRETENDED TO BE ME MA WHEN YOUR ONE WAS ASKIN' DID I HAVE PERMISSION FROM ME MA. STOP! THE THINGS WE USED TO GET UP TO! ANYWAY, THESE ARE SOME OF ME ALL-TIME FAVOURITE STUN HUN PIERCINGS.

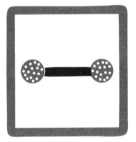

BELLY BUTTON - LOOKS UNREAL WITH A CROP TOP

TONGUE - GREAT FOR MEETIN' FELLAS

NECK BAR - LOOKS MASSIVE WHEN YE HAVE YOUR HAIR UP IN A BUN

NOSE - STUNNIN' WITH A RING

TRAGUS - LOOKS STUNNIN' WHEN YE HAVE SHORT HAIR

MADONNA - GIVES YE THA' BEAUTY SPOT YE NEVER HAD

# YIZZER PHONE

YIZZER PHONE IS THE ULTIMATE ACCESSORY, SWEAR! I WOULDN'T
BE CAUGHT DEAD WITH A BLOKIA NOWADAYS, I'D BE SCARLEH.
IT'S DEADLY FOR CHECKIN' FACEBOOK EVERY SECOND OF THE
DAY WHILE YE WORRY THA' SOMEONE'S SEEN YOUR MESSAGE
AND HASN'T WRITTEN BACK IN 5 HOURS.

THESE ARE ME FAVOURITE APPS TO USE. I USE MOST OF THEM
EVERY DAY, ESPECIALLY WHATSAPP FOR HAVIN' A RANT WITH THE GIRLOS
OR CHECKIN' TO SEE IF SOMEONE'S ALIVE AFTER A MAD NIGH' OUT.
INSTAGRAM IS ME GO-TO APP FOR TAKIN' A GOOD SELFIE WHILE I HAVE
PINTEREST FOR MAKIN' WEDDIN' BOARDS FOR ME AND MY ANTO'S
WEDDIN'. SWEAR THOUGH, EVEN THOUGH I WOULDN'T WANT A BLOKIA NOW
I MISS MAKIN' ME OWN TONES AND BEATIN' TANYA'S SCORE ON SNAKE.
THOSE WERE THE DAYS.

GRAND FOR A GOOD
CREEP ON YOUR
FELLA'S EX

ALRIGH' FOR SLAGGIN'
CELEBRITIES AND ACTIN'
THE BOLLIX

UNREAL FOR FILTERS
BUT EASY TO GET
CAUGHT CREEPIN'

DEADLY FOR ORGANISIN'
A PARTY OR WEDDINGS
AN' ALL

GAS FILTERS FOR
HAVIN' A LAUGH

FOR MESSAGIN'
YIZZER FRIENDS
AND GOIN' ON A
MAD ONE

# NIKITA'S
## TOP MASSO ACCESSORIES

HERE ARE SOME OF ME FAVOURITE ACCESSORIES AND THINGS THA' I LOVE. THERE WAS TOO MANY TO CHOOSE FROM BUT THESE ARE ME TOP ONES.

FLUFFY FRAME WITH ANTO'S MUG

MEDALLION RING WITH ME INITIAL

LIPS PHONE CASE I FOUND IN THE JAX IN THE BLACKER

ME NAILS WHEN THEY'RE FRESHLY DONE

# WHA' DOES YOUR BAG SAY ABOUT YOU?

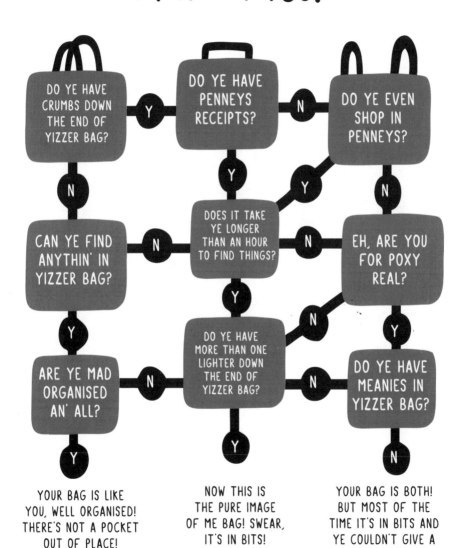

DO YE HAVE CRUMBS DOWN THE END OF YIZZER BAG?

Y

DO YE HAVE PENNEYS RECEIPTS?

N

DO YE EVEN SHOP IN PENNEYS?

N

Y

CAN YE FIND ANYTHIN' IN YIZZER BAG?

N

DOES IT TAKE YE LONGER THAN AN HOUR TO FIND THINGS?

N

EH, ARE YOU FOR POXY REAL?

Y

Y

N

ARE YE MAD ORGANISED AN' ALL?

N

DO YE HAVE MORE THAN ONE LIGHTER DOWN THE END OF YIZZER BAG?

N

DO YE HAVE MEANIES IN YIZZER BAG?

Y

Y

N

YOUR BAG IS LIKE YOU, WELL ORGANISED! THERE'S NOT A POCKET OUT OF PLACE!

NOW THIS IS THE PURE IMAGE OF ME BAG! SWEAR, IT'S IN BITS!

YOUR BAG IS BOTH! BUT MOST OF THE TIME IT'S IN BITS AND YE COULDN'T GIVE A RAT'S!

# ME FAVOURITE CLOTHES TO WEAR

HERE'S A MASSO SELECTION OF ALL ME FAVOURITE CLOTHES FOR
EVERYDAY WEAR, AS WELL AS GOIN' 'OUT OUT' BITS TOO. THESE ARE THE
ESSENTIALS FOR YIZZER 'STUN HUN' WARDROBE AND A MUST HAVE IF YE
WANT TO BE AS MASSIVE AS ME. SWEAR! COULDN'T LIVE WITHOUT ME
FLUFFY SOCKS FROM PENNEYS. THA' MASSIVE FEELIN' WHEN YE PUT ON
A FRESH PAIR, STOP! HEAVEN!

# RUNNERS

VERDY GOOD
FOR SKETCHIN'
FROM THE GARDA

ALRIGH' FOR HIDIN' MONEY
UNDER THE INSOLE

MAX

GRAND FOR WALKIN'
THE SHOPS

I'D BE LOST WITHOUT ME AIR MAX. I PREFER BUYIN' RUNNERS OVER
HEELS ANY DAY. MY ANTO GOT ME THESE FOR ME BIRTHDAY LAST
YEAR AND THEY STILL LOOK BRAND NEW. IT'S IMPORTANT WHEN
YOU'RE STUNNIN' TO LOOK AFTER YIZZERSELF AND ALWAYS HAVE
YOUR RUNNERS PURE WHITE. THERE'S NOTHIN' WORSE THAN HAVIN'
DIRTY WHITE RUNNERS, STOP! ME NERVES.

# TRACKSUITS

### TRACKSUIT TIPS

NEVER WEAR WITH HEELS, NO MATTER WHA' THE MAGAZINES TELL YE. IT'S POXY ROTTEN.

TUCK YIZZER BOTTOMS INTO YOUR SOCKS SO YE CAN LEGGIT WITHOUT TRIPPIN' AND GOIN' FLYIN' ON YIZZER FACE.

A MATCHIN' TRACKIE IS ESSENTIAL TO BE PURE MASSIVE. I LOVE ME ADIDAS TRACKIE AND ME CAMOUFLAGE ONE TOO. THEY'RE GRAND FOR WHEN YOU'RE JUST CHILLIN' IN THE GAFF AND NEED TO RUN TO THE SHOPS. ME AND TANYA HAVE MATCHIN' ONES BUT WE NEVER WEAR THEM ON THE SAME DAY, STOP! HATE WHEN THA' HAPPENS.

# PURJAMMERS

## GOIN' OUT

## STAYIN' IN

THE DIFFERENCE BETWEEN GOIN' OUT AND STAYIN' IN PURJAMMERS IS THA' ONE IS FOR WEARIN' TO BED AND ONE IS FOR RUNNIN' TO THE SHOPS OR HANGIN' AROUND IN. IT'S A STUN HUN SIN TO WEAR YOUR STAYIN' IN PJ'S WHEN YOU'RE GOIN' OUT! IT'S PURE ROTTEN. I REMEMBER WHEN ME AND TANYA USED TO WEAR OUR GOIN' OUT ONES UNDER OUR SKIRTS IN SCHOOL TO KEEP US WARM – KIP WAS POXY FREEZIN' ALL THE TIME.

# PADDED BRA

EXTRA PADDIN' FOR PANCAKES

SWEAR! I LOVE GETTIN' MATCHIN' BRA SETS IN PENNEYS. THEY DO HAVE MASSIVE ONES IN WHEN IT GETS CLOSER TO THE SUMMER. YE CAN NEVER HAVE TOO MANY BRAS. I KNOW SOME PEOPLE DON'T WEAR THEM, AND GOOD FOR THEM, BUT I HAVE TO, OTHERWISE WHEN I'M LEGGIN' IT FOR A BUS ME DIDDIES WILL CLOCK ME IN THE JAW AND I'LL BE KO'D ON THE GROUND.

# BOMBER JACKET

## BOMBER TIPS

NEVER WEAR FULLY ZIPPED UP, YE ONLY LOOK LIKE A SAP. LOOKS MASSIVE WITH LEGGINS AND NIKE AIRS.

NOTHIN' BEATS A DECENT BOMBER JACKET! THE ONLY THING IS EVERY POX IS WALKIN' AROUND TOWN IN ONE NOW, SO IF I WAS YOU I'D GET A MAD COLOURED ONE ON THE INTERNET SOMEWHERE AND WHEN SOMEONE SAYS, 'AH THAT'S MASSIVE, HUN. WHERE DID YE GET THA'?' JUST SAY, 'DON'T KNOW, HUN. ANTO'S MA GOT IT FOR ME ON HOLIDAYS'. SORTED! LEAST YOU'LL STAND OUT FROM THE CROWD, IN A GOOD WAY OBVIOUSLY.

# LEGGINS

## LEGGIN' TIPS

MAKE SURE THE LEGGINS ARE GOOD QUALITY SO YE CAN'T SEE YOUR KNICKERS THROUGH THEM.

NEVER TRUST A HUN WITH SEE-THROUGH LEGGINS, JUST SAYIN'.

LEGGINS ARE THE HOLY GRAIL OF HUN CLOTHIN', EVERYONE OWNS AT LEAST ONE PAIR OF LEGGINS. THEY GO WITH EVERYTHIN' AND YE CAN EVEN WEAR THEM AS TROUSERS. YE ALWAYS HAVE SOME POX MOANIN' SAYIN', 'YOU'RE NOT SUPPOSED TO WEAR THEM AS TROUSERS', AND I'M ALWAYS LIKE, 'LUV, I'LL WEAR WHATEVER I POXY WANT'.

# SLOGAN TEES

DON'T GET A
T-SHIRT WITH A
ROTTEN SLOGAN,
GET SOMETHIN' THA'
REPRESENTS YOU LIKE
'MASSO', 'STUN HUN',
'HUNREAL', 'RIDE', ETC.

ME WARDROBE IS FULL OF T-SHIRTS. I USUALLY GET THEM IN NEW
LOOK OR FOREVER 21, THEY ALWAYS HAVE MASSIVE ONES IN THERE.
THEY LOOK STUNNIN' WITH LEGGINS AND JEANS AND THEY'RE
HANDY SOMETIMES IF YOU'RE GOIN' ON A NIGH' OUT AND YOU DON'T
WANT TO GET MAD DRESSED UP. THA' REMINDS ME, ME POX OF A
SISTER TOOK A LEND OF ONE LAST WEEK AND I NEVER GOT IT BACK.

# CROP TOPS AND BANDEAUS

MASSIVE WITH
HIGH-WAISTED JEANS

SWEAR! WISH I HAD NO DIDDIES COS I'D BE WEARIN' THESE ALL
THE TIME! WOULD YE STOP! THEY GO MASSIVE WITH ANYTHIN'
AND YE CAN WEAR THEM CASUALLY OR ON A NIGH' OUT. THEY'RE
LOVELY FOR FESTIVALS AND PERFECT FOR YOUR HOLLIERS.

# FLUFFY SOCKS

THA' SOFT FEELIN' WHEN YE PUT ON A FRESH PAIR! STOP, MASSIVE!

NO HUN IS COMPLETE WITHOUT ABOUT A MILLION ODD PAIRS OF FLUFFY SOCKS FROM PENNEYS IN THEIR BEDROOM. THEY'RE THE PERFECT CHILL-OUT ACCESSORY AND ARE PERFECT FOR THE WINTER WHEN IT'S BLEEDIN' BALTIC OUT. BUT WHEN YE STEP IN SOMETHIN' WET OFF THE FLOOR? IT'S ROTTEN! THE WHOLE VIBE IS RUINED. I DO GO MAD WHEN ANTO SPILLS HIS CAN AND DOESN'T CLEAN UP AFTER HIMSELF.

# PLATFORMS

GIVES YE A BOOST
IF YOU'RE SMALL
LIKE ME

I ONLY REALLY WEAR HEELS WHEN I'M GOIN' OUT FOR A BOP WITH THE GIRLS. I NEVER LEARN THOUGH COS I DO ALWAYS BE IN BITS BY THE END OF THE NIGH'. ALSO, IF YE DON'T WANT ANY FELLAS CHATTIN' YE UP ON A NIGH' OUT, JUST WEAR KITTEN HEELS. SWEAR! IT'S LIKE FASHION CONTRACEPTION.

# BODYCON

AHH, THE BODYCON. KEEPIN' THEM ROLLS WHERE THEY BELONG, BACK IN THE BAKERY. THIS IS ME FAVOURITE GOIN' OUT DRESS, AND EVERY HUN NEEDS A LITTLE BLACK DRESS IN THEIR WARDROBE. I'VE ONLY WORN IT TWICE NOW THOUGH. I NEVER REALLY WEAR THE SAME THINGS OUT COS THEN IT LOOKS LIKE YE HAVE NO CLOTHES WHEN PEOPLE TAG YE IN PICS ON FACEBOOK.

# HOOP SHORTS

PERFECT FOR
FESTIVALS AN' ALL

SEE THESE LIL' BEAUTS? THEY'RE MASSIVE AREN'T THEY? I ALWAYS
WEAR THESE IN THE SUMMER, BUT ON NIGHTS OUT LIKE. WOULDN'T
BE WALKIN' CENTRA OR ANYTHIN' IN THEM, THA' WOULD BE A BIT
MUCH. IMAGINE GOIN' TO BUY A BREAKFAST ROLL IN THEM! SCARLEH.

# GOIN' SHOPPIN'

EVERYONE DESERVES TO TREAT THEMSELVES EVERY NOW AND AGAIN,
AND FOR ME IT'S NEARLY EVERY WEEK, WOULD YE STOP! I'LL BE SHOWIN'
YIZ HOW TO COPE WITH HEAD MELTERS WHILE SHOPPIN', YIZ KNOW THE
ONES! CHANGIN' ROOM HOGGERS AND SUNDAY STROLLERS AND THE POXY
REST. I'LL ALSO BE TELLIN' YIZ THE THINGS YOUR FELLA SAYS WHILE
SHOPPIN' AND WHA' THE POX ACTUALLY MEANS, AND HOW TO RESPOND
TO A COMPLIMENT LIKE A TRUE HUN.

# WHERE TO GO SHOPPIN'

HENRY STREET IS THE BEST PLACE TO SHOP IN TOWN FULL STOP!
YE HAVE EVERYTHIN' THERE AND YE DON'T EVEN NEED TO WALK
FAR. THEY HAVE THE BEST PENNEYS BY FAR ON MARY STREET
AND THERE'S TWO SHOPPIN' CENTRES ON THE SAME POXY ROAD!
IT DOESN'T GET ANY BETTER THAN THIS. IF YOU'RE LOOKIN' FOR
SOMETHIN' A BIT POSHER, THEY HAVE ARNOTTS UP THE ROAD AND
THERE'S A MASSIVE TOPSHOP IN THERE TOO.

# RESPONDIN' TO COMPLIMENTS

THERE ARE TWO MAIN RESPONSES WHEN SOMEONE SAYS TO YE, 'AH YE LOOK STUNNIN' OR 'THA' TOP IS MASSIVE, WHERE DID YE GET IT?' AND THE MOST COMMON ONE IS, 'THANKS HUN, PENNEYS'. EVERY HUN LOVES A GOOD BARGAIN IN PENNEYS, 2 EURDO EARRINGS, 3 EURDO SLIPPERS AND WHATEVER ELSE YE CAN GET YIZZER HANDS ON. I LIVE IN THIS SHOP, SWEAR! TANYA IS BARRED THOUGH COS SHE TRIED TO ROB FLUFFY SOCKS WEARIN' A CAMO TRACKIE - THE SAP THOUGHT SHE WAS INVISIBLE!

● THANKS HUN, PENNEYS

● AH THE HACK OF ME, WOULD YE STOP

# HOW TO AVOID HEAD MELTS WHILE SHOPPIN'

ME WHEN ME
HEAD'S WRECKED IN TOWN

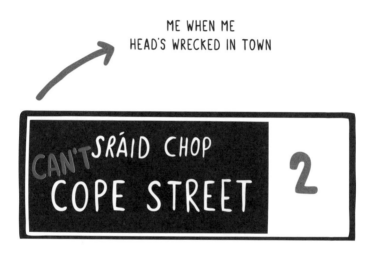

THERE'S NOTHIN' WORSE WHEN YE GO TO TOWN ON A SATURDAY AND THE PLACE IS FULL OF ANNOYIN' SAPS GETTIN' IN YIZZER WAY AND HOLDIN' YE UP WHEN YOU'RE TRYIN' TO GET IN AND OUT OF SOMEWHERE IN A HURRY! I DO BE SNAPPIN'. I REMEMBER ONE POX WAS IN THE DRESSIN' ROOM FOR AN HOUR. I WAS LIKE, 'EH, YOU WATCHIN' REPEATS OF EASTENDERS IN THERE OR SOMETHIN LUV? YOU'RE TAKIN' POXY AGES.' STOP! WAS GOIN' ON A MAD ONE. ANYWAY! ON THE NEXT PAGE I'M GONNA TELL YE HOW YE CAN AVOID THESE KINDS OF DZZZOOPPES!

## DRESSIN' ROOM HOGGERS

WHEN SOMEONE IS TAKIN' AGES, CALL THEM OUT ON IT AND THE POX ALWAYS HURRIES UP

## SUNDAY STROLLERS

I LOVE WALKIN' MAD SLOW!

IF SOME POX WALKS IN FRONT OF YE AND STOPS, JUST KEEP ON WALKIN', HUN

## SCREAMIN' KIDDIES

MAAAA!!

BLOCK OUT THE SOUND OF SCREAMIN' KIDS BY NOT GOIN' INTO PENNEYS ON A SATURDAY

## SELFIE TAKERS

WHEN SOMEONE IS TAKIN' SELFIES IN FRONT OF A MASSIVE JACKET YE WANT, PHOTOBOMB THE SAPS

# SHOPPIN' WITH FELLAS

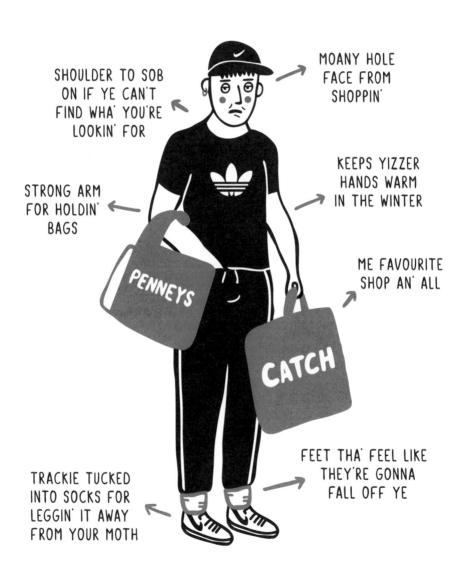

# THINGS FELLAS SAY WHILE SHOPPIN' (TRANSLATED)

YEAH THAT'S LOVELY ('MON, HURRY UP)

YEAH GRAND (ME POXY FEET)

IT'S NEARLY 8 O'CLOCK (THE MATCH IS STARTIN')

YEAH I WILL IN A MINUTE (MAYBE IF I DON'T SHE'LL FORGET)

AH LOOK! THERE'S MCDONALD'S (STARVIN'!)

# SHOPPIN' WITH GIRLS

GRAND FOR KEEPIN'
EXTRA SHOPPIN'

3 EURDO,
PENNEYS

THE 'CURVED
ARM' STUN
HUN POSE

STUNNIN' CROP TOP
I GOT ON ME HOLLIERS

MASSIVE JEANS I
GOT LAST WEEK
IN PENNEYS

ABOUT A MILLION
BAGS FROM
DIFFERENT SHOPS

THE 'KILBARRACK
KARDASHIAN' LEG
POSE

# THINGS GIRLS SAY WHILE SHOPPIN' (TRANSLATED)

YEAH IT'S ALRIGH' (THAT'S ROTTEN)

THAT'S MASSIVE (THAT'S UNREAL)

IT'S ME BIRTHDAY NEXT WEEK, JUST SAYIN'

(IF YE DON'T GET ME THA' BAG I'LL POXY SNAP)

EH, YOU FOR REAL?

(TAKE THA' OFF YE)

THAT'S ROTTEN

(I WANT THA' DON'T BUY IT)

# SHOPPIN' FAILS

AWH STOP! I HATE WHEN YOU'RE AFTER BEIN' IN TOWN ALL DAY AND YE EITHER CAN'T FIND ANYTHIN' TO WEAR OR WHA' YOU'VE BOUGHT LOOKS ROTTEN WHEN YE TRY IT ON AT HOME. THESE ARE SOME OF ME OWN SHOPPIN' FAILS, THERE'S NOTHIN' WORSE. WHEN THIS HAPPENS YE HAVE TO REMEMBER YOU'RE MASSIVE AND THE CLOTHES WERE JUST MADE WRONG - NOT YOUR FAULT LIKE.

## BIG DIDDIES

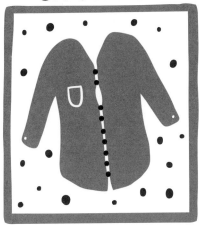

WHEN YE HAVE BIG DIDDIES AND THERE'S A GAP BETWEEN THE BUTTONS ON A MASSIVE SHIRT

## SMALL LEGS

WHEN HIGH-WAISTED JEANS ARE STILL TOO LONG ON YE COS YOU'RE ONLY SMALL

## TINY FEET

WHEN YOU'RE A SIZE 3 AND THE SHOPS NEVER HAVE YIZZER SIZE IN

## HOOP HASSLE

WHEN YE GET A MASSIVE DRESS AND YOUR HOOP KEEPS FALLIN' OUT OF IT

# NIKITA'S
## SHOPPIN' LIST

FLUFFY SOCKS

RUNNERS FROM THE ILAC

LEGGINS FROM PENNEYS

A MASSIVE DRESS

JEANS FROM TOPSHOP

A CAN OF DUTCH

# WHA' DID YE BUY IN TOWN?

MONTH YE WERE BORN

FIRST LETTER OF YIZZER NAME

| | | |
|---|---|---|
| JAN STUNNIN' | A LEGGINS | N CAKE FROM THUNDERS |
| FEB MASSO | B FOOT SCRUB | O GIMP MASK |
| MAR HUNREAL | C FANNY CREAM | P PAIR OF KNICKERS |
| APR LOVELY | D TOILET SCRUBBER | Q PILE CREAM |
| MAY ROTTEN | E VIBRATOR | R HAIRY SOAP |
| JUN WEIRD | F FANNY WAX | S SPICEBAG JOHNNIES |
| JUL STUN HUN | G EXTENSIONS | T RONNIE CREAM |
| AUG NICE | H CHICKEN FILLETS | U STICK-ON EYEBROWS |
| SEP ALRIGH' | I BRILLO PADS | V DIDDIE TASSELS |
| OCT EXPENSIVE | J VODKA | W HOOP ENHANCER |
| NOV CHEAP | K VEGETABLES | X NIPPLE CREAM |
| DEC BROWN THOMAS | L HEARIN' AID | Y CAT FOOD |
| | M FAKE MICKEY | Z CILLIT BANG |

# GOIN' OUT FOR A BOP
## FOR A BOP
### WITH THE GIRLS

IT'S FRIDAY NIGH' AGAIN AND EVERYONE IS BUZZIN' TO GET OUT INTO
TOWN FOR A BOP WITH THE GIRLOS, AND WHA' BETTER WAY TO START
OFF THE NIGH' THAN ESSENTIAL PRE-DRINK MESSIN' WITH YOUR HUNS.
I'LL ALSO BE SHOWIN' YIZ PLACES TO HEAD TO AFTER YIZZER
PRE-DRINKS AND WHERE TO HIDE YIZZER NAGGIN SO THE BOUNCERS
WON'T FIND IT. AIN'T NO PARTY LIKE A 'STUN HUN' PARTY, WHA? GERRRUP!

# GETTIN' READY

GETTIN' READY FOR A NIGH' OUT CAN TAKE AGES. WELL, IT DOES FOR ME ANYWAYS AND ANYONE ELSE WHO WANTS TO LOOK MASSIVE. YE HAVE TO MANAGE YIZZER TIME ACCORDINGLY, OTHERWISE YOU'LL BE LATE GETTIN' INTO TOWN AND THE ONLY THING YOU'LL HAVE TIME FOR WILL BE A 6-PIECE NUGGET MEAL AND A TAXI BACK HOME AGAIN, WOULD YE STOP! ON THE NEXT PAGE YOU'LL SEE THE ORDER I GET MESELF READY IN.

## SHOWER

HAVE A SHOWER, NO ONE LIKES
A SMELLY POX. YIZ ARE FOOLIN'
NO ONE WITH YIZZER SCENTED
ALWAYS PADS.

## TAN

AFTER YIZZER SHOWER, APPLY
YOUR TAN. NO BETTER FEELIN'
THAN WHEN YOUR TAN IS EVENLY
SPREAD ON YIZZER LEGS.

## NAILS

DOIN' YIZZER NAILS THE DAY OF
GOIN' OUT IS MAD RISKY. I DO
ALWAYS END UP RUSHIN' MINE
AND THEN THE GLUE GOES POXY
EVERYWHERE.

## MAKE-UP

LAST BUT NOT LEAST, DO YIZZER
MAKE-UP, COS YE CAN ALWAYS
STRAIGHTEN YIZZER HAIR WHILE
HAVIN' A DRINK AFTER YE TROW
YIZZER CLOTHES ON.

# PRE-DRINKS

STRESS OF GETTIN'
READY, NEED A DRINK

FINALLY GOT
ME LASHES ON

AH IT'S ONLY
9, IT'S GRAND

MASSO
WINE!

JAYSUS! IT'S
MAD LATE

THE POXY TAXI IS
OUTSIDE, 'MON WILL
YIZ!

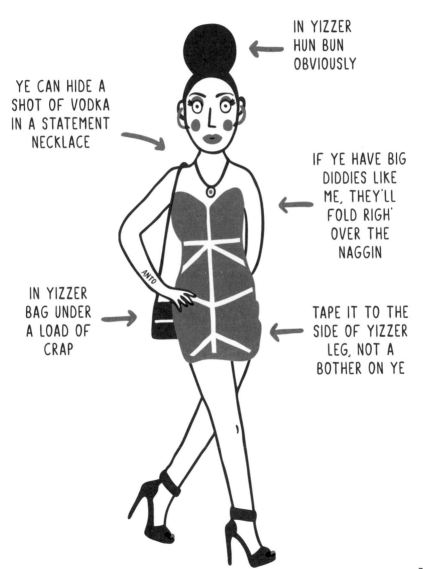

# WHAT'S IN YOUR GOIN' OUT BAG?

I ALWAYS HAVE ME ESSENTIALS FOR GOIN' OUT. I LIKE TO BRING ME LIPSTICK COS IT DOES COME OFF AFTER A FEW DRINKS. MONEY FOR GRUB AFTERWARDS IS THE MOST IMPORTANT. I DO BRING A FEW JOHNNIES WITH ME AS WELL BECAUSE IT'S BETTER TO BE SAFE THAN SORRY! IN 9 MONTHS I WANT TO BE IN IBIZA NOT THE ROTUNDA, THANKS VERDY MUCH.

# HOW TO AVOID GETTIN' IN PICS WHEN YOU'RE ROTTEN

IF YOU'RE NOT IN THE MOOD TO GET IN PICS FOR THE NIGH' THEN YOU'RE NOT ON YOUR OWN. SOMETIMES WE JUST DON'T FEEL MASSIVE, AND THAT'S ALRIGH' FROM TIME TO TIME, HUN. I SUGGEST PUTTIN' A PAPER BAG OVER YIZZER HEAD SO NO ONE BOTHERS YE. NO ONE WANTS A POX WITH A PAPER BAG ON THEIR HEAD TO RUIN THEIR SQUAD PHOTO.

# GETTIN' THE BUS
## (INTO TOWN)

GETTIN' THE BUS INTO TOWN FOR A NIGH' OUT IS EVERY YOUNG
ONE'S RIGH' OF PASSAGE. ONLY MASSIVE HUNS SIT AT THE
BACK OF THE BUS, BECAUSE THEN YE CAN SEE ALL THE FELLAS
STRUTTIN' UP THE AISLE AND MAKE EYE CONTACT WITH THEM.
AND HERE, YE NEVER KNOW WHEN DAVID BECKHAM'S GONNA
STRUT DOWN THA' BUS AISLE. YE HAVE TO BE READY, IT'S A
ONCE IN A LIFETIME OPPORTUNITY. IF YE SIT UP THE FRONT
YOU'RE EITHER A BORIN' POX OR A TOURIST.

# GETTIN' A TAXI
## (IN AND OUT OF TOWN)

TAXI MEN IN DUBLIN ARE MAD SOUND FOR GETTIN' YE HOME SAFE. SOMETIMES THEY WAIT FOR YE TO GET IN THE DOOR AND YE JUST GIVE THEM THE THUMBS UP TO SAY 'I'M IN, PAL'. I DO BRING A PLASTIC BAG WITH ME INTO TOWN OR ASK YOUR MAN TO PULL OVER IF I FEEL THE NUGGETS COMIN' BACK UP. IT WRECKS ME HEAD THOUGH WHEN SOME OF THEM ARE LIKE, 'I'M NOT RACIST BUT...' IF YOU'RE NOT RACIST DON'T BE GOIN' ON A RANT, PAL. NOW HURRY UP, MY ANTO'S WAITIN' ON ME AT HOME.

# PUBS

ME FAVOURITE PUBS TO GO TO AT THE WEEKEND

GAMES    GOOD PINTS    BANTER

## NORTH

THE BACK PAGE 👄 👄 🎲
THE BLACK SHEEP 👄 🎲 👍
THE COCK AND BULL 👄 👍
THE GRAND SOCIAL 👄 👍
WIGWAM 👄 👍

## SOUTH

P. MAC'S 👄 🎲 👍
THE GLOBE 👄 👍
WHELAN'S 👄 👍
THE BERNARD SHAW 👄 👍
AGAINST THE GRAIN 👄 🎲 👍

# CLUBS

ME FAVOURITE CLUBS TO GO TO AT THE WEEKEND

BOP — COCKTAILS — BANTER

## NORTH

THE LIVING ROOM ♫♫Y😋
THE WRIGHT VENUE ♫YY😋
THE CHURCH ♫ YY😋
THE BLACKER - RIP ♫Y😋
PANTI BAR ♫Y😋😋

## SOUTH

PLAY NIGHTCLUB ♫Y😋
PYG ♫YY😋
CAPITOL ♫YYY😋
SIN ♫♫Y😋
THE PALACE ♫Y😋

# MUNCHIES
## (BLEEDIN' STARVIN')

IF THE LINE IS TOO BIG IN MCDONALD'S, MAKE SURE THA' YOU'VE STOCKED UP ON MUNCHIES THE DAY BEFOREHAND SO YE HAVE A BIT OF GRUB THERE WHEN YE GET HOME. NOTHIN' SOAKS THE DRINK UP LIKE A MASSIVE PACK OF ME FAVOURITES, MEANIES. I LIKE TO HAVE A REFRESHER BAR AFTER THEM COS IT FRESHENS YE UP AFTER THE CRIPS, AND THEN A CAN OF 7UP BEFORE BED SO I CAN PREPARE FOR ME HANGOVER THE NEXT DAY.

# WHAT'S YOUR SESSION MOTH NAME?

**MONTH YE WERE BORN**

**FIRST LETTER OF YIZZER NAME**

| | | | |
|---|---|---|---|
| JAN STUNNIN' | A THUNDER FLAPS | N RAISIN NIPPLES |
| FEB MASSIVE | B CODDLE DIDDIES | O TWISTED DIDDIES |
| MAR HEYA | C PICKLE POX | P FURRY ARSE |
| APR ROTTEN | D SASSY SAP | Q ACRYLIC HOOP |
| MAY STUN HUN | E TASSEL TICK | R BISCUIT BOP |
| JUN YOLO | F RUBBER FLAPS | S CURRY TOES |
| JUL MASSO | G MEANIE BREATH | T GOLDY GEE |
| AUG MIGHTY | H SAGGY SAUSAGE | U MOULDY FLAPS |
| SEP SWEATY | I FLAPPY HOOP | V TWINKLE DIDDIES |
| OCT STICKY | J HAIRY HOOP | W CLATTER FLAPS |
| NOV SALTY | K THUNDER HOOP | X SCALDY SAP |
| DEC MOIST | L SCAREDY NIPPLES | Y SLASH GASH |
| | M PUDDIN' TWERK | Z FANCY FANNY |

# TALKIN' TO FELLAS

SWEAR! I MET MY ANTO ON THE INTERNET AN' ALL AND WE'RE A MATCH MADE IN HEAVEN. JUST WISH THE POX WOULD HURRY UP AND PUT A RING ON IT, THE TICK. ANYWAYS! I'LL BE SHOWIN' YIZ THE WAYS OF LOVE AND HOW TO FIND THE PERFECT FELLA ONLINE. SEE THA' TINDER APP AS WELL? I HAVE IT PURE SUSSED! YOU'LL BE SORTED FINDIN' A TOP BLOKE AFTER THIS CHAPTER - NOT THA' AN INDEPENDENT HUN NEEDS ONE, JUST IF YOU'RE LOOKIN', RIGH'!

# TINDER AND ONLINE DATIN'

THERE'S NO SHAME IN FINDIN' YIZZER TRUE LOVE ONLINE, IT'S THE
FUTURE AND THAT'S WHA' EVERYONE DOES NOW. SURE LOOK AT ME
AND ANTO, WE MET ONLINE AND WE'RE PERFECT. BUT NOT EVERYONE IS
PERFECT AND YE HAVE TO KEEP AN EYE OUT FOR THE FAKE PROFILES. ME
FRIEND TANYA'S ALWAYS GETTIN' POXY CAT-FISHED. SHE EVEN THOUGHT
SHE WAS MEETIN' MR TAYTO. FEEL SORRY FOR HER SOMETIMES I DO.

# FAKE PROFILES

SPEAKIN' OF TANYA GETTIN' CAT-FISHED, HERE'S SOME OF THE FELLAS SHE THOUGHT SHE WAS SEEIN'.

MICKA GICKNAH

SPUDDY O'REILLY

SOUND GARDA

JASON BYRNE'S MASSO HAIR

# DEAL BREAKERS

NOPE

A REAL UNICORN ↓

PADDY MOONEY

THERE ARE JUST SOME THINGS THAT MAKE ME GO 'NO' STRAIGHT AWAY WHEN I SEE A FELLA'S PROFILE. ONE OF THOSE THINGS IS WHEN HIS PROFILER IS OF HIS CAR, HIS HORSE OR IF HE'S IN A PICTURE WITH A MILLION OTHER FELLAS AND YE CAN'T TELL WHICH ONE THE POX IS. WRECKS ME HEAD, SWEAR.

# TIPS FOR DATES

DON'T BE GOIN' ON AN' ON ABOUT YIZZER EX, FELLAS HATE THA'

I MISS HIM

UR ALRI

IN CASE YE SEE TOM HARDY OUT HAVIN' A BOP AND HE WANTS TO MEET YE COS YOU'RE MASSIVE, XOX

PLAY HARD TO GET IF YE THINK HE'S A BEAUT!

DON'T BE EATIN' ONIONS OR ANYTHIN' THA' SMELLS ROTTEN

TOP TIP

# ME DREAM BLOKE

NOW WE'RE TALKIN', WHA'? A GIRL CAN POXY DREAM, RIGH'!
SWEAR THOUGH, TOM HARDY IS JUST MASSIVE, ISN'T HE? TELLIN'
YE, IF I SEEN TOM HARDY WALKIN' THROUGH THE ILAC AND HE
SAID "MON NIKITA, LET'S RUN AWAY", I'D BE JUST LIKE 'I ALREADY
HAVE ME BAG PACKED PAL, BOOK A HAILO THERE AND WE'LL GO
OFF TO KUSADASI HUN'. NO OFFENCE TO MY ANTO OR ANYTHIN'.
I LOVE HIM TO BITS, BUT IT'S TOM HARDY LIKE.

# HOW YE KNOW IF HE'S 'THE ONE'

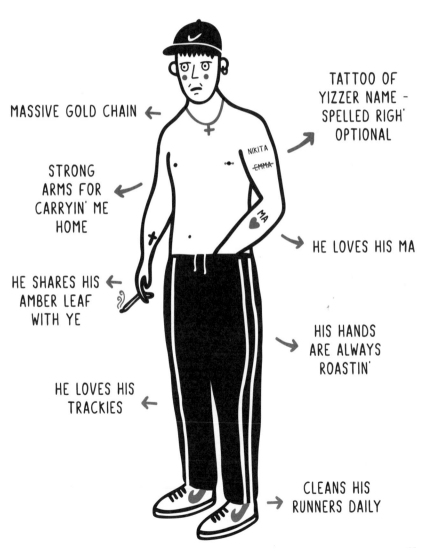

MASSIVE GOLD CHAIN ←

STRONG ARMS FOR CARRYIN' ME HOME ←

HE SHARES HIS AMBER LEAF WITH YE ←

HE LOVES HIS TRACKIES ←

TATTOO OF YIZZER NAME – SPELLED RIGH' OPTIONAL

NIKITA
EMMA

MA

→ HE LOVES HIS MA

HIS HANDS ARE ALWAYS ROASTIN'

CLEANS HIS RUNNERS DAILY

# WHEEL OF DOOM

THIS IS THE WHEEL OF DOOM. WE ALL THINK OF THESE THINGS BEFORE WE GO TO MEET A FELLA, BUT THE REALITY IS THA' EVERYONE IS DIFFERENT AND YOU'RE NOT GOIN' TO KNOW WHA' HE'S LIKE UNTIL YE MEET THE POX, SO TAKE A CHILL PILL AND RELAX. THE ONLY PERSON LETTIN' YE DOWN IS YIZZERSELF BECAUSE YOU'RE BUILDIN' IT UP IN YOUR HEAD, LUV. TAKE IT STEP BY STEP.

# CHECKLIST

ME PRINCE

BIG SHOULDERS ☑

BIG MICKEY ☑

BIG HANDS ☑

NOT A SAP ☑

ONCE YE HAVE MET YOUR PERFECT FELLA DO UP A CHECKLIST AND SEE IF HE TICKS ALL THE BOXES. IF HE DOES, WELL THEN HE'S A KEEPER HUN, JUST SAYIN'. ONLY DO A CHECKLIST AFTER YOU'VE MET WITH THEM AN' ALL, COS IF YE JUST DO IT BEFORE YOU KNOW SOMEONE THEN YE MIGHT BE BUILDIN' YIZZERSELF UP FOR SOMETHIN' THAT'S JUST NOT THERE! THERE NEEDS TO BE A SPARK.

# IN THE BEDROOM

THESE ARE SOME OF ME FAVOURITE THINGS TO USE IN THE BEDROOM. TAKE NOTE.

HANDCUFFS SO YOUR FELLA CAN'T RUN AWAY WHEN YE WANT TO WATCH EX ON THE BEACH

IF YE HAVE CRUSTY ROTTEN NIPPLES, THESE TASSELS WILL HIDE THEM AND MAKE YE MASSIVE AGAIN

SPICE UP YIZZER LIFE AND FANNY WITH SOME SPICEBAG LUBE

IF YE DON'T HAVE A FELLA ONE OF THESE YOKES ARE GRAND

# DYIN' FOR A DRINK

SOMETIMES WHEN WE GO OUT WE WAKE UP WITH THE FEAR. 'WHO DID I WHATSAPP?' 'DID I REALLY RIDE SOMEONE ON A ROBBED PUSH BIKE WITH ONE WHEEL?' THESE ARE QUESTIONS WE ASK OURSELVES EVERY WEEKEND. THE ANSWER IS 'YEAH LUV, YE WERE THAT BAD', BUT NIKITA'S HERE TO FIX IT! I'LL BE SHOWIN' YIZ HOW YE KNOW WHEN IT'S TIME TO GO HOME AND HOW TO SURVIVE THE HANGOVER FROM HELL THE NEXT MORNIN'!

# THE DEVIL

# HOW TO HAVE A GOOD ONE
## (WITHOUT OVERDOIN' IT)

PRE-DRINKS

IN BITS =

SHOTS

THE THING THA' DOES HAVE ME IN BITS THE NEXT DAY IS IF I PRE-DRINK AND THEN HAVE SHOTS WHEN I'M OUT, STOP! I DO BE IN A HOOP. YOU'RE BETTER OFF DOIN' EITHER ONE OR THE OTHER BECAUSE IT'S NOT WORTH IT. IF YE DRINK A GLASS OF WATER BETWEEN YIZZER DRINKS AND YOU'RE NOT ALREADY LOCKED, SWEAR, SAVES YE A HANGOVER THE NEXT DAY AND YE WAKE UP BRAND NEW, PAL.

# NIKITA COCKTAILS

THESE ARE SOME OF ME HOMEMADE CONCOCTIONS I DO MAKE FOR ME AND THE GIRLS BEFORE WE HEAD OUT INTO TOWN. MASSIVE THEY ARE.

DOLE DAY GABBANA

YE ALRIGH' HUN?

ROTTEN POX

A SHOT OF
YOUR MICKEY

FANCY FANNY

SEX ON THE
HONDA CIVIC

# DRINKS

THESE ARE SOME OF ME FAVOURITE DRINKS TO HAVE WHEN I'M OUT.

CAN OF DUTCH     BULMERS     WKD BLUE

REKORDERLIG     JAGER BOMB     VODKA AND COKE

# HOW YE THINK YE LOOK

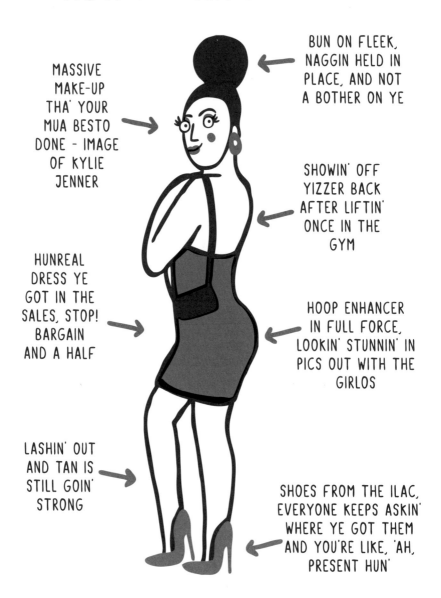

MASSIVE
MAKE-UP
THA' YOUR
MUA BESTO
DONE – IMAGE
OF KYLIE
JENNER

BUN ON FLEEK,
NAGGIN HELD IN
PLACE, AND NOT
A BOTHER ON YE

SHOWIN' OFF
YIZZER BACK
AFTER LIFTIN'
ONCE IN THE
GYM

HUNREAL
DRESS YE
GOT IN THE
SALES, STOP!
BARGAIN
AND A HALF

HOOP ENHANCER
IN FULL FORCE,
LOOKIN' STUNNIN' IN
PICS OUT WITH THE
GIRLOS

LASHIN' OUT
AND TAN IS
STILL GOIN'
STRONG

SHOES FROM THE ILAC,
EVERYONE KEEPS ASKIN'
WHERE YE GOT THEM
AND YOU'RE LIKE, 'AH,
PRESENT HUN'

# HOW YE ACTUALLY LOOK

TROW YIZZER
HANDS IN
THE AIR AND
WAVE 'EM LIKE
YE JUST DON'T
CARE, YE TICK

YERRRRRRR
GERRRUPPP!
MANIAC - ME
TUNE!

TROWIN' SOME
MASSIVE
SHAPES AND
WRECKIN' THE
BOUNCERS'
HEADS

YOU'RE ON A
MAD ONE BUT
YE STILL HAVE
YIZZER
SPICEBAG MONEY
SO IT'S ALL
GOOD

DRESS
IS POXY
RUINED!
STILL HAVE
THE TAG ON
IT THOUGH,
SOUUUND!

BILLY ELLIOT, WHA'!!

BREAKIN' IN THE NEW
SHOES YOU'LL PROBABLY
NEVER WEAR AGAIN

# WHEN TO CALL IT A NIGH'

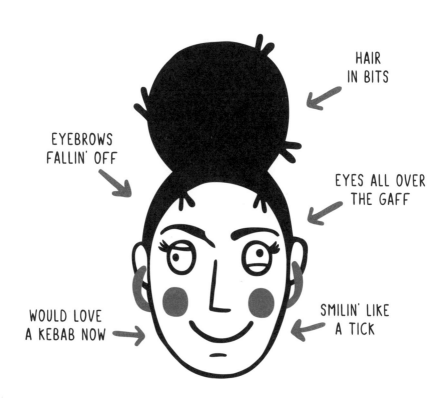

HAIR IN BITS

EYEBROWS FALLIN' OFF

EYES ALL OVER THE GAFF

WOULD LOVE A KEBAB NOW

SMILIN' LIKE A TICK

SOMETIMES WHEN YOU'RE HAVIN' A WHOPPER TIME YE DO FORGET WHEN ENOUGH IS ENOUGH AND YE GO OVER THE TOP. IT ALWAYS LEADS TO YE HAVIN' NOT ONLY A BAD HANGOVER BUT WAKIN' UP HAVIN' TO EXPLAIN YIZZERSELF TO EVERYONE AND THERE'S NOTHIN' WORSE! THESE ARE SOME OF ME TELL-TALE SIGNS THA' I HAVE TO GO HOME TO ME BED.

# DRUNK TEXTIN'

SWEAR! WHEN I'M OUT TANYA ALWAYS TAKES ME PHONE AWAY FROM ME
COS I DO BE TEXTIN' ANTO'S EX AND EVERYTHIN'! IT'S NOT NICE BEIN'
LIKE THA' BUT WHEN YE HAVE A BIT OF DRINK ON YE THAT'S WHEN YE
TURN INTO A LIL' KEYBOARD WARRIOR. IF YE FIND YIZZERSELF GOIN'
ON A MAD ONE TEXTIN', STOP AND THINK IF YE CAN, COS YOU'LL ONLY
BE SCARLEH WHEN YE WAKE UP THE NEXT DAY AND EVERYONE DOES
BE TALKIN' ABOUT YE. THERE'S NOTHIN' MASSIVE ABOUT STARTIN' ON
SOMEONE FOR NO REASON AT ALL.

# HANGOVER HELL

HAIR IS ROTTEN, STOP!

HEAD IS BANGIN'

TRYIN' TO FIND THE WILL TO POXY LIVE

CURRY BLOB FROM LAST NIGH'

NEW PURJAMMERS

WET FLUFFY SOCKS, FML

STOP! I CAN'T COPE WHEN I HAVE A HANGOVER, I DO BE SOBBIN' DOWN THE PHONE TO ANTO ASKIN' HIM TO BRING ME FOOD. THERE'S NOTHIN' MASSIVE ABOUT BEIN' HUNGOVER TO BITS. SEE, WHEN I TAKE ME EYEBROWS OFF NO ONE SEES ME - ON HANGOVER DAYS SNAPCHAT IS OFF LIMITS COS I'M PURE ROTTEN SO DON'T EVEN BOTHER. OH! ME NAME ON SNAPCHAT IS ROTTENPOX. ADD ME, HUN.

# HANGOVER CURES

THESE WILL SORT YIZZER HEADS RIGH' OUT WHEN YE HAVE THE WORST HANGOVER IN THE WORLD.

TRY STAYIN' IN BED ALL DAY WATCHIN' DISNEY MOVIES.

TIE A PAIR OF LEGGINS ROUND YIZZER HEAD TO GET RID OF THA' BANGIN' HEADACHE.

TOAST IS ME LIFE SAVER WHEN I'M IN BITS, THA' AND WATER SORT ME RIGH' OUT.

5 O'CLOCK, SPICEBAG O'CLOCK - TIME TO SOAK UP THIS HANGOVER WITH A CURRY.

# THINGS WE SAY THE DAY AFTER A SESSION

AH THE THINGS WE DO TELL OURSELVES AFTER A NIGH' OUT AND THEN WE DO THE SAME THING NEXT WEEKEND. WOULD YE EVER STOP! I NEVER LEARN - SAME STORY, DIFFERENT DAY.

# WHO'S YOUR DRINKIN' WING WOMAN?

**MONTH YE WERE BORN**

**FIRST LETTER OF YIZZER NAME**

JAN ME STUN HUN

FEB ME GIRLO

MAR ME NO.I HUN

APR ME PARTNER IN CRIME

MAY ME ONE AN' ONLY

JUN ME BESTO

JUL ME HUNZO

AUG ME MAD YOKE

SEP ME HEAD BANGER

OCT ME LIL' DIAMOND

NOV ME STAR FROM AFAR

DEC ME LIL' BEAUT

A OPRAH

B IGGY AZALEA

C RIHANNA

D MILEY CYRUS

E BEYONCÉ

F TAYLOR SWIFT

G MILA KUNIS

H BRITNEY, BITCH

I NICKI MINAJ

J GWEN STEFANI

K ELLEN DEGENERES

L MEGAN FOX

M J LO

N MISSY ELLIOTT

O KATY PERRY

P LINDSAY LOHAN

Q PARIS HILTON

R KIM KARDASHIAN

S CAITLYN JENNER

T ADELE

U LADY GAGA

V ARIANA GRANDE

W RITA ORA

X JESSIE J

Y FLEUR EAST

Z MEGHAN TRAINOR

# HOW YE KNOW IF A FELLA LIKES YE

SOME PEOPLE CALL ME ... OH, WHAT'S HIS NAME AGAIN? THA' FAT MAN
BABY IN THE NAPPY. CUPID!! THAT'S THE ONE. TO BE HONEST, I DON'T
KNOW WHY I DON'T HAVE ME OWN 'DEAR NIKITA' SECTION IN THE STAR,
COS I'M A LOVE GURU, SWEAR DOWN! I'LL TEACH YIZ THE TELL-TALE
SIGNS OF WHEN A FELLA LIKES YE, AS WELL AS TRANSLATE THE HINTS
HE LEAVES IN HIS TEXTS.

# TEXT TRANSLATION

SWEAR! NOTHIN' WRECKS ME HEAD MORE THAN WHEN YOU'RE TEXTIN'
A FELLA YE LIKE AND YOU'VE NO IDEA IF THE POX EVEN LIKES YE.
SOUND FAMILIAR? WELL, YIZ ARE IN LUCK BECAUSE I'M A PRO AT
TRANSLATIN' TEXTS FROM FELLAS AND BEIN' ABLE TO TELL IF THEY
LIKE YE. HERE ARE SOME TELL-TALE SIGNS THA' A FELLA FANCIES YE.

WHAT'S UP? → WILL YE MEET ME?

YE SINGLE? → COS I WANT TO MEET YE

DO YE LIKE CHICKEN? → IF YE DON'T LIKE NANDO'S WE CAN'T BE TOGETHER

YE THERE? → I CAN SEE YOU'RE ONLINE!

# HE'S MAD SOUND

DEFO
NOT
ROBBED

MY ANTO IS ALWAYS BRINGIN' ME FLOWERS. EVEN IF THEY'RE FROM HIS
POX OF A NEIGHBOUR'S GARDEN, IT'S THE THOUGHT THA' COUNTS. AND
THA' AULD ONE HAS SOME MASSIVE FLOWERS IN HER GARDEN, STOP!
ANYWAY, THE FIRST SIGN OF TELLIN' IF A FELLA LIKES YE IS IF HE'S
NICE TO YE.

# HE CHOOSES YE OVER THE XBOX

FELLAS LOVE PLAYIN' THE XBOX AND IF YOU'RE SEEIN' A POX WHO'S BEEN PLAYIN' THE XBOX THE LAST 3 HOURS AND HAS FORGOTTEN YOU'RE EVEN THERE, THEN FORGET IT! YE CAN DO BETTER HUN, CHIN UP AN' ALL THA'. A REAL MAN WILL CHOOSE YOU OVER GTA ANY DAY.

# HE TALKS ABOUT YE TO HIS MATES

A FELLA DOESN'T USUALLY TALK TO HIS MATES ABOUT A BIRD UNLESS IT'S GETTIN' SERIOUS AND HE REALLY LIKES HER. UNFORTUNATELY YOU'LL PROBABLY NEVER KNOW IF HE'S TALKIN' TO HIS FRIENDS ABOUT YE, UNLESS YE GET HIS PHONE AND CHECK HIS MESSAGES. BUT THE MOST IMPORTANT THING IN A RELATIONSHIP IS TRUST HUN, AND YOU'D BE BREAKIN' IT BY DOIN' THIS. IT'S NOT WORTH IT, LUV.

# HE'S ALWAYS SMILIN' LIKE A SAP

WOULD YE LOOK AT THE
BIG SMILEY HEAD ON HIM

IF A FELLA IS ALWAYS SMILIN' AROUND YE IT'S AN OBVIOUS SIGN THA'
HE THINKS YOU'RE MASSIVE, EITHER THA' OR HE'S UP TO SOMETHIN'.
MY ANTO IS ALWAYS TRAPPIN' ME UNDER THE COVERS AND FARTIN'
ON ME. FELLAS DO THA' WHEN THEY LIKE YE AS WELL, IT'S ROTTEN.

# HE'S GOT A PIC OF YE ON HIS WALL

IF HE HAS A PIC OF YE ON HIS WALL OR IF HE HAS HIS FACEBOOK PROFILER AS A PICTURE OF YOU AND HIM, THEN YE KNOW THA' HE THINKS YOU'RE PURE MASSIVE. JAYSUS, YE MIGHT AS WELL UPDATE YIZZER RELATIONSHIP STATUS ON FACEBOOK AT THIS STAGE AND LET ALL OF YIZZER FRIENDS KNOW IF THEY DON'T ALREADY. MAKE SURE TO CHANGE YIZZER RELATIONSHIP STATUS 20 TIMES A YEAR TO LET EVERYONE KNOW WHEN YIZ ARE FIGHTIN'.

# HE TAKES YE OUT FOR FOOD

YE KNOW A FELLA LIKES YE WHEN HE TAKES YE OUT FOR A ROMANTIC MEAL AND BUYS YE SOMETHIN' THAT'S NOT ON THE EURDO SAVER MENU. THAT'S TRUE LOVE RIGHT THERE, HUN.

# HE COMPLIMENTS YE ALL THE TIME
## (WHEN HE WANTS SOMETHIN')

DID I TELL YE YE LOOK STUNNIN'?

AWH STOP! MY ANTO IS FOREVER SAYIN' TO ME, 'AH, YE LOOK LOVELY TODAY HUN, DID YE GET YIZZER HAIR DONE?' AND I'M ALWAYS LIKE, 'NO BABE, I JUST WASHED IT.' THEN THE POX DOES ASK ME FOR SOMETHIN', FOR EXAMPLE, 'YE WOULDN'T HAVE A LEND OF A TENNER FOR A CHIPPER WOULD YE?'

# HE WATCHES GEORDIE SHORE WITH YE

YE KNOW A FELLA IS MAD INTO YE WHEN HE WATCHES GEORDIE SHORE WITH YE OVER THE FOOTBALL. THAT'S SOME COMMITMENT RIGHT THERE THA' IS! EVERY FELLA WILL TELL YE EVERY TIME THERE'S A MATCH ON, 'IT'S A REALLY IMPORTANT MATCH, CAN'T MISS IT'.

# HE TRIES TO IMPRESS YE

REV
REV

UNCE
UNCE

ALL ANTO'S MATES THINK THEY'RE MAD REVVIN' THEIR CIVICS UP THE
ROAD IN FRONT OF ALL THE MOTHS. THIS IS ANOTHER TELL-TALE SIGN
A FELLA IS INTO YE, BUT IT ALSO MAKES THEM LOOK LIKE A TICK AS
WELL. I'VE NEVER SEEN THIS WORK ON ANY GIRLS IF I'M HONEST WITH YE.
JUST BECAUSE YOU'RE ABLE TO REV YOUR CAR UP AND DOWN THE ROAD
DOESN'T MEAN YE HAVE A BIG MICKEY, HUN. CALM DOWN, IT'S AFTER 8,
YOUR MA'S LOOKIN' FOR HER CAR BACK.

# NETFLIX AND CHILL

IF YE DON'T HAVE NETFLIX THEN THE DODGY BOX WILL DO.
THIS ONE IS SELF-EXPLANATORY AND I DON'T THINK YE NEED ME
ADVICE AT THIS STAGE. IF YIZ HAVE 'WATCHED' A WHOLE SERIES
ON NETFLIX IN A NIGH' WELL THEN YIZ ARE PRACTICALLY MARRIED.
CONGRATULATIONS, YE TICK.

# MASSO
# HACKS

RIGH', SO EVERY HUN HAS HER OWN 'MASSO HACKS' TO MAKE HER DAY-TO-DAY LIFE A BIT EASIER. DO YOU THINK I GET ME POXY RUNNERS THIS WHITE WITH BABY WIPES? DO I LOOK LIKE I HAVE 5 HOURS TO SPARE SCRUBBIN' ME RUNNERS A DAY? THE ANSWER IS 'NO!' COS I'M A BUSY WOMAN AN' ALL. ANYWAYS! IN THIS CHAPTER I'LL BE SHARIN' ME MOST VALUABLE HUN LIFE HACKS WITH YIZ, SO TAKE NOTE BECAUSE THESE WILL SORT YIZZER LIVES RIGH' OUT, SWEAR.

# CLEAN YIZZER RUNNERS WITH TOOTHPASTE

NOW, IF YOU'RE LOOKIN' TO GET YIZZER RUNNERS PURE WHITE, THE SECRET IS TO USE SOME TOOTHPASTE WITH SOME WHITENING IN IT! ALL YE NEED IS AN OLD TOOTHBRUSH AND SOME TOOTHPASTE AND YIZZER MANKY RUNNERS. AFTER YE SCRUB THEM WITH THE TOOTHPASTE AND SOME WATER, SWEAR! THEY LOOK BRAND NEW, PAL! THERE'S NOTHIN' MORE COMFORTIN' THAN HAVIN' FRESH RUNNERS.

# FLAT 7UP WILL LEAVE YE FEELIN' BRAND NEW

WE ALL KNOW THA' IF YE FEEL A BIT ROPEY, THE BEST THING TO DO IS WHACK SOME 7UP INTO THE POT, BOIL IT UP AND GET IT INTO YE! THIS WORKS WONDERS IF YOU'RE DYIN' WITH A HANGOVER AND CAN'T EAT ANYTHIN'. SWEAR, ANTO MAKES IT FOR US ALL THE TIME. IT WORKS FOR THE KIDDIES TOO IF THEY'RE SICK. THA' AND DRY TOAST ARE THE IRISH REMEDIES TO MAKE YE FEEL BETTER.

# USE A POOR BOX AS A PIGGY BANK

YE EVER LEAVE A 50 AROUND THE GAFF AND IT GOES WALKIN'?
HAPPENS IN MY GAFF ALL THE TIME. THE BEST PLACE TO HIDE YIZZER
MONEY IS IN A POOR BOX! WHA' POX IS GONNA GO ROOTIN' FOR A
SCORE IN A POOR BOX? NOBODY! COS THEY'RE ALWAYS FULL WITH
PENNIES AND CHIPPER MONEY SO IF THEY WANT THEIR DINNER LATER
THEY WON'T TOUCH IT COS THEY KNOW WHAT'S GOOD FOR THEM.
CHARITY STARTS AT HOME AN' ALL.

# HEAT UP A SLICE OF PIZZA WITH AN IRON

ANTO SHOWED ME THIS AND I THOUGHT HE WAS TAKIN' THE PISS
BUT IT ACTUALLY WORKS! AND IT'S DEADLY FOR WHEN YOU'RE
HUNGOVER TO BITS AND DON'T WANT TO MOVE FROM YIZZER BED.
GET OUT THE DOMINO'S FROM LAST NIGH' AND BLAZE THA' SLICE, HUN!

# WEIGH YIZZERSELF WITH ONE LEG

BEEN CHEATIN' ON SLIMMIN' WORLD? NO BOTHER! TO MAKE YIZZERSELF FEEL BETTER, WEIGH YIZZERSELF WITH ONE LEG AND YOU'LL BE GUARANTEED TO HAVE LOST AT LEAST HALF A STONE. THEN YE WON'T FEEL AS BAD MILLIN' THA' CURRY INTO YE LATER! STOP!

# TOILET ROLL IN THE JAX

WHEN YOU'RE GOIN' FOR A NUMBER 2 THERE'S NOTHIN' WORSE THAN THE TOILET WATER SPLASHIN' YIZZER ARSE WHEN THA' BEAT DROPS. PUT SOME BOG ROLL AT THE BOTTOM OF THE JAX AND YE WON'T HAVE THIS PROBLEM ANYMORE. YIZZER ARSE WILL BE AS DRY AS GANDHI'S SANDALS.

# OPEN A BOTTLE WITH A SPOON

IF YE HAVE NO BOTTLE OPENER AND YOU'RE SNAPPIN', USE A SPOON OR THE END OF A LIGHTER TO POP THE LID OFF THE BOTTLE. WORKS JUST AS WELL AS A BOTTLE OPENER WOULD. SORTED PAL!

# HIDIN' MUNCHIES
## FROM YIZZER FELLA

WHENEVER ME POX OF A FELLA COMES HOME FROM THE PUB HE ALWAYS EATS ALL ME MUNCHIES AND THEN I HAVE NOTHIN' LEFT THE NEXT DAY. THE BEST PLACE TO HIDE THEM IS BEHIND A TOWEL IN THE WASHIN' MACHINE, BECAUSE GOD KNOWS THE POX HAS NEVER TOUCHED THE THING IN HIS LIFE.

# SAVE YIZZER BATTERY

IS YIZZER BATTERY ALWAYS DYIN'? WELL, TRY BUYIN' THE REAL CHARGER FOR YIZZER PHONE COS THE FAKE ONES MESS UP THE BATTERY. STAYIN' OFF FACEBOOK FOR MORE THAN 5 MINUTES SAVES YIZZER BATTERY TOO. I TRIED AND LASTED 3 MINUTES OFF THE THING. IT'S VERDY HARD TO DO, ESPECIALLY WHEN SOMEONE SENDS YE A MESSAGE.

# SPRAYIN' HAIRSPRAY ON YIZZER FACE

SPRAY A LITTLE BIT OF HAIRSPRAY ON YIZZER FACE TO SET YIZZER MAKE-UP. THIS WORKS WONDERS, ESPECIALLY IF YOU'RE NEARLY SOBBIN' WATCHIN' EASTENDERS ON THE WAY OUT. YOUR MAKE-UP STAYS INTACT AND YE LOOK MASSIVE FOR THE REST OF THE NIGH'.

# FRESH WATER IS THE
## SECRET TO A MASSO CUPPA

DID YE EVER HAVE A MASSIVE CUP OF TEA IN SOMEONE'S GAFF AND THEN YE MAKE ONE IN YOUR OWN AND IT TASTES LIKE THE LIFFEY? WELL, THE SECRET TO A MASSIVE CUP OF TEA IS TO PUT FRESH WATER IN YIZZER KETTLE EVERY TIME BEFORE BOILIN' THE POXY THING. ME NANNY TAUGHT ME THA' BEAUT OF A TRICK.

# WHA' HAPPENS WHEN
## YE DON'T SEND ON CHAINMAIL?

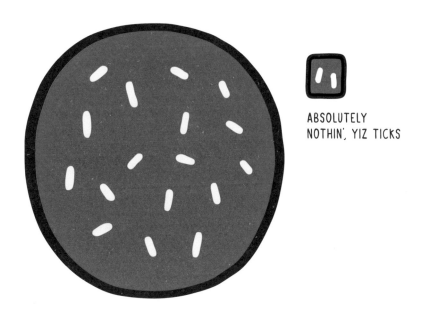

ABSOLUTELY
NOTHIN', YIZ TICKS

WHEN A POX SENDS YE A CHAINMAIL, WRITE BACK SAYIN' IT'S A LOAD OF
POX AND THEN THE NEXT DAY TELL THEM YOU'VE BEEN CURSED. THEY'LL
NEVER SEND YE CHAINMAIL AGAIN COS THEY'LL BE BRICKIN' IT IN CASE
YE CURSE THEM AS WELL!

# FAMILY SESSIONS AND UGLY CONFESSIONS

SOMETIMES IN LIFE WE HAVE TO GO TO FAMILY EVENTS THA' WE
DON'T WANT TO GO TO COS THEY'RE FULL OF SAPS AND SMALL TALK.
WELL, FOR A LIMITED TIME ONLY I'LL BE SHOWIN' YE HOW TO AVOID
THE ANNOYING POXES, AS WELL AS WHA' TO SAY WHEN YOUR FELLA
FINALLY PROPOSES AND WHA' TO PACK FOR YIZZER SUMMER HOLIDAYS.
STOP! WOULD LOVE TO BE GOIN' TURKEY THIS YEAR - THA' POX ANTO
BETTER WIN ON THE HORSES.

# FAMILY PARTIES
## (STORY OF ME POXY LIFE)

ME AT FAMILY PARTIES

WHENEVER I GO TO ONE OF ME FAMILY'S PARTIES OR GET TOGETHERS I ALWAYS END UP TALKIN' TO THE SAPS IN THE CORNER WHEN ME FRIENDS ARE OVER THE OTHER SIDE OF THE POXY ROOM. IT'S ALRIGH', I'M JUST STUCK TALKIN' TO TERESA OR WHATEVER HER NAME IS TELLIN' ME ALL ABOUT HOW HER GREGORY IS TAKIN' UP SWIMMIN' LESSONS. SORRY LUV, I'VE NO IDEA WHO YE ARE BUT YOU'RE WRECKIN' ME BUZZ, SWEAR!

# TYPES OF PEOPLE
## (IN YIZZER FAMILY)

THE 'KNOW IT ALL'

THE 'SOUND UNCLE'

THE 'MAD AUNTY'

THE 'ONE WHO
LOVES A BIT
A DRAMA'

THE 'NANNY WHO
SPEAKS HER MIND'

THE 'TRAINEE
HAIRDRESSER'

THE 'I GOT ALL
A'S IN MY LEAVING'

THE 'DEL BOY'

THE 'MOAN BAG WITH
A BIT OF GOSSIP'

# AWKWARD CONVOS

SOMETHIN' THA' WRECKS ME HEAD EVEN MORE AT THESE PARTIES IS WHEN YE SEE SOMEONE YE HAVEN'T SEEN IN YEARS AND THEY START PASSIN' OUT ALL THE COMPLIMENTS: 'AH ARE YE PREGNANT, LUV? IT'S ABOUT TIME', 'HEARD YE DONE BAD IN THE LEAVIN', BETTER LUCK NEXT TIME'. EH, DONE ME LEAVIN' 5 YEARS AGO PAL, THERE IS NO NEXT TIME AND I ALREADY HAVE A DIPLOMA IN TOLERATIN' TICKS LIKE YOU ON A DAILY BASIS. CHEEK OF YE, JOG ON PAL.

# SHORT REPLIES
## (TO GET OUT OF BORIN' CONVOS)

# GOIN' AWAY WITH THE FELLA

TOP TIPS FOR HAVIN' A MASSIVE HOLIDAY WITH YIZZER FELLA.

DELETE ALL YIZZER PICS SO YE HAVE SPACE FOR TAKIN' SOME ON YIZZER HOLLIERS.

TAKE SOME PICS OF YIZ MEETIN' IN FRONT OF A SUNSET AND PUT IT UP ON FACEBOOK.

HOLD HANDS SO OTHER POXES ON HOLIDAYS KNOW HE'S YOUR FELLA AND NO ONE ELSE'S.

TAG YOUR FELLA IN EVERY STATUS AND CHECK INTO EVERYWHERE, EVEN THE AIRPORT JAX.

# WHA' TO PACK FOR YIZZER HOLLIERS

YE HAVE TO HAVE A MASSIVE BIKINI THA' SHOWS OFF YIZZER FIGURE AND MAD SUNGLASSES THA' NO ONE ELSE HAS. I ALWAYS BRING FACTOR 50 AWAY WITH ME COS I'M A PALE POX AND TURN INTO A LOBSTER. A NAGGIN WILL CALM THE NERVES ON THE PLANE OVER AS WELL! AND YE SEE THA' BEACH TOWEL? YE CAN WRAP UP ALL YIZZER SMOKES AN' ALL COMIN' BACK, NOT A BOTHER ON YE!

# WHA' TO SAY WHEN THE POX FINALLY PROPOSES

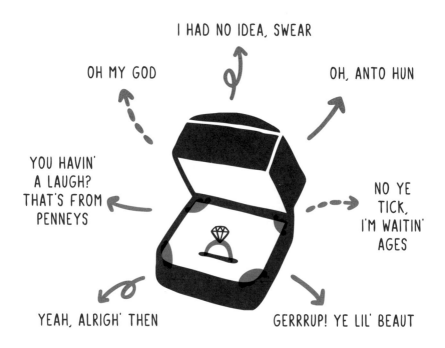

I HAD NO IDEA, SWEAR

OH MY GOD

OH, ANTO HUN

YOU HAVIN'
A LAUGH?
THAT'S FROM
PENNEYS

NO YE
TICK,
I'M WAITIN'
AGES

YEAH, ALRIGH' THEN

GERRRUP! YE LIL' BEAUT

IF YOU'RE WITH YOUR FELLA AGES AND HE HASN'T PROPOSED YET, WHY DON'T YE THINK OF WHA' TO SAY IF HE DOES COS THEN YE CAN ACT MAD SHOCKED AND SWEAR THA' YE DIDN'T FIND THE RING IN HIS POCKET TWO MONTHS AGO? BUT WHATEVER YIZ DO, CHECK YIZZER FOOD BEFORE YE EAT IT. MY ANTO PUT MINE IN A SPICEBAG AND I WAS IN THE HOSTIPAL FOR AGES, WAS SOBBIN'. HAD TO WAIT UNTIL IT CAME OUT AGAIN SO HE COULD PROPOSE PROPERLY.

# DROPPIN' HINTS
## (FOR PRESENTS)

THIS IS HOW YE DROP HINTS LIKE A PRO. PAY ATTENTION, HUN.

'ME ENGAGEMENT FINGER'S
FREEZIN' ANTO, SWEAR.'

'AWH, SEEN A MASSIVE PAIR OF
RUNNERS IN LIFESTYLE THE
OTHER DAY.'

'ALL ME FRIENDS HAVE AN
ALEX AND ANI BRACELET
EXCEPT ME, I'M SCARLEH.'

'ME EXTENSIONS BLEW
AWAY AND FELL INTO THE
LIFFEY, SOBBIN' I AM ANTO.'

# WHA' NOT TO SAY AT A CHRISTENIN'

STOP! CHRISTENINS ARE SPECIAL DAYS FOR PRINCES AND PRINCESSES SO THE LAST THING YE WANT TO DO IS SAY THE WRONG THING TO THE MA AND DA AND RUIN THE POXY DAY, COS YOU'LL ALWAYS BE REMEMBERED AS THA' YOUNG ONE WHO RUINED MIA ROSE'S CHRISTENIN'. YE DON'T WANT THA' OVER YOUR SHOULDERS FOR THE REST OF YIZZER LIFE, TRUST ME.

# GIRLO
# CODE

RIGH', SO IN EVERY GROUP OF HUNS THERE'S A GIRLO CODE. A LOT OF IT IS COMMON SENSE TO BE HONEST WITH YE, BUT SOME PEOPLE JUST DON'T KNOW WHA' TO DO IN CERTAIN SITUATIONS. LIKE, IF SOMEONE HAS A MAKE-UP RONNIE AND THEY'RE CHATTIN' UP A FELLA THE LAST 20 MINUTES, HOW DO YE BREAK THE POXY NEWS? WELL, NIKITA'S HERE TO TEACH YE THE GIRLO CODE.

# ALWAYS REMEMBER YOU'RE MASSIVE, EVEN IN A CRISIS!

IN A CRISIS, ALWAYS REMAIN CALM AND REMEMBER THA' YOU'RE MASSIVE. THIS WILL GET YE THROUGH THE TOUGH TIMES, ESPECIALLY WHEN YOU'VE SPENT AN HOUR TAKIN' A SELFIE ONLY TO REALISE THA' THERE'S NO POXY WIFI, SNAPPIN'!

# EX—FELLAS ARE
# OFF LIMITS

EX-FELLAS ARE A NO-GO FOR OBVIOUS REASONS. IT'S VERDY BAD
TO GO OFF WITH A HUN'S EX, ESPECIALLY IF HE BROKE HER HEART
AN' ALL. IF YE WANT TO MEET SOMEONE'S EX-FELLA AND YOU'RE
CLOSE FRIENDS WITH THEM, I'D ASK IF I WAS YOU, JUST SAYIN'.

# YE ALWAYS HELP YIZZER MATES

YOU'RE ALWAYS THERE FOR YIZZER FRIENDS AND YE HAVE THEIR BACKS WHEN SOME POX IS ANNOYIN' THEM WHEN YIZ ARE OUT TRYIN' TO HAVE A GOOD ONE. YE ALSO HAVE THEIR BACKS IN OTHER WAYS TOO, LIKE WHEN THEY'RE TOO HUNGOVER TO GO THE SHOP TO GET A CHICKEN FILLET ROLL.

# YE KEEP GUARD OF YOUR BESTO'S PHONE

THERE'S NOTHIN' WORSE THAN WHEN YE HAVE A GO AT SOMEONE, ESPECIALLY WHEN YOU'RE TEXTIN' THEM COS YE COULD SAY ANYTHIN' AND IT COULD COME ACROSS WAY WORSE, EVEN IF YE DIDN'T MEAN IT AN' ALL. I ALWAYS MIND TANYA'S PHONE COS SHE'S ALWAYS TEXTIN' PEOPLE WHEN SHE'S LOCKED.

# SPICEBAGS FIX EVERYTHING

HAD A BREAK-UP? LOST YIZZER JOB? OR MAYBE A SEAGULL JUST TOOK
A SHIT ON YE AND ROBBED YIZZER CHICKEN FILLET ROLL? A SPICEBAG
WILL SORT YE OUT AND HELP YE FORGET ABOUT THE HORRIBLE DAY
YE JUST HAD. THEY'RE NOT EVEN BAD FOR YE REALLY COS THEY HAVE
VEGETABLES, SO IT'S LIKE ONE OF YIZZER 5 A DAY.

# ALWAYS BE HONEST

IF YE GOT SOMETHIN' TO SAY, THEN SAY IT TO ME FACE

ALWAYS BE HONEST WITH YIZZER FRIENDS AND YOU'LL NEVER HAVE ANYTHIN' TO REALLY WORRY ABOUT. AS THE SAYIN' GOES, DATIN' BACK TO 1801, 'IF YE GOT SOMETHIN' TO SAY, THEN SAY IT TO ME FACE' - WISE AULD ONE.

# YE AGREE THA' BIEBER HAS SOME ABSOLUTE CRACKERS OUT

NOT EVEN MESSIN', I USED TO THINK BIEBER WAS A POX AND THA' ONLY 12-YEAR-OLDS LIKED HIM BUT, SWEAR, HE'S AFTER BELTIN' OUT SOME ABSOLUTE CRACKERS OF TUNES LATELY! THE BLOKE CAN DO NO WRONG IN MY EYES.

# TELL SOMEONE IF THEY HAVE A MAKE-UP RONNIE
## (BUT MAKE SURE IT'S JUST A MAKE-UP RONNIE)

IF SOMEONE YE KNOW HAS A MAKE-UP RONNIE OR A TIDEMARK, YE SHOULD LET THEM KNOW AS SOON AS POSSIBLE COS THERE'S NOTHIN' WORSE THAN WALKIN' AROUND ALL DAY THINKIN' YOU'RE MASSIVE WHEN YE LOOK LIKE A TICK.

# DON'T BE A SAP

YE CAN'T
SIT WITH
US, YE TICK

IF ONE OF THE HUNS STARTS STRUTTIN' AROUND THINKIN' THEY'RE
BETTER THAN ALL OF YIZ, IT'S YOUR DUTY TO KNOCK THE POX DOWN
A PEG. IF THEY DON'T LISTEN THEN TELL THEM, 'WE ONLY WEAR
PENNEYS ON WEDNESDAYS SO YE CAN'T SIT WITH US'.

# YE DON'T NEED A FELLA
## WHEN YE GOT NUTELLA

IF YE DON'T HAVE A FELLA THEN YOU'RE ALRIGH' COS
YE HAVE NUTELLA, AND NUTELLA IS MASSIVE.

# SHARIN' IS CARIN'

MINE

YOURS

IF YE GET A 6-PIECE NUGGET MEAL, IT'S CUSTOMARY TO GIVE YOUR FRIEND 3 OF THE NUGGETS. THAT'S JUST THE RULES HUN, SORRY!

# NEVER TELL SECRETS

IT'S BANG OUT OF ORDER TO GO AROUND TELLIN' A HUN'S SECRETS.
WHEN SOMEONE TELLS YE A SECRET IT'S CALLED A POXY SECRET
FOR A REASON. NOTHIN' WORSE THAN WHEN YE THINK YE KNOW
SOMEONE AND THEY'VE BEEN BITCHIN' BEHIND YIZZER BACK. WELL
LUV, I CAN SEE RIGHT THROUGH YE. YOU'RE AS TRANSPARENT AS
YOUR LEGGINS, PAL!

# EXTRA BITS

THIS SECTION IS FULL OF EXTRA BITS AND PIECES LIKE SOAP DRINKIN'
GAMES, STUNNIN' HOROSCOPES AND QUIZZES LIKE 'WHAT'S YOUR STUN
HUN NAME?' THERE'S EVEN A 'DEAR NIKITA' SECTION WITH REAL-LIFE
PROBLEMS SOLVED BY YOUR ONE AND ONLY NO.I STUN HUN, ME! NIKITA.
ENJOY, YIZ TICKS!

# DEAR NIKITA
### REAL-LIFE PROBLEMS AN'ALL

## SEX DREAM RUINED ME POXY LIFE

HEYA NIKITA,

HOPE YE CAN HELP ME, HUN. I HAD A SEX DREAM ABOUT TOM HARDY AND I TOLD ME FELLA, AND NOW HE'S NOT TALKIN' TO ME BECAUSE HE CONSIDERS IT CHEATIN'. THINGS HAVEN'T BEEN GOIN' WELL IN THE BEDROOM. I DON'T KNOW WHAT TO DO!

NIKITA: NOT BEIN' FUNNY LUV, BUT YOUR FELLA SOUNDS LIKE A POX. I DON'T KNOW HOW YOU'VE BEEN PUTTIN' UP WITH HIM FOR SO LONG IF I'M BEIN' HONEST WITH YE. HAVIN' A SEX DREAM ISN'T CHEATIN' ON SOMEONE, YOU'RE POXY ASLEEP SO HOW ARE YE MEANT TO CONTROL YIZZERSELF, YE KNOW? I HAVE DREAMS ABOUT TOM HARDY TOO, BUT DOES THA' MEAN HE'S CHEATIN' ON ME WITH YOU? NO, NO IT DOESN'T, COS IT'S ONLY A BLEEDIN' DREAM. IF I WAS YOU I'D BE TELLIN' THA' FELLA OF YOURS TO COP ON AND THA' HE DOESN'T KNOW A GOOD THING WHEN HE SEES IT.

HEYA HUN

FREE FANNY PAD* IN NEXT ISSUE *NOT USED

168

**WHY DOES ME SON ALWAYS HAVE ODD SOCKS DOWN THE SIDE OF HIS BED?**

HEYA KITA,

I'M JUST WONDERIN' WHY ME SON HAS LOADS OF ODD SOCKS DOWN THE SIDE OF HIS BED, LUV?

NIKITA: ASK YIZZER FELLA HUN, HE'LL TELL YE WHY. DON'T ASK YIZZER SON THOUGH COS HE'LL BE SCARLEH!

**SOBBIN' ALL WEEK !**

HEYA NIKITA,

I DON'T KNOW WHAT'S WRONG WITH ME, I CAN'T STOP SOBBIN' AFTER PEGGY MITCHELL DIED IN EASTENDERS. WAS VERY SAD AN' ALL.

NIKITA: AH WOULD YOU EVER STOP. IT'S NOT EVEN REAL, YE TICK.

**I'M POXY SNAPPIN' !**

HEY NIKITA,

I'M SNAPPIN'! NEVER BEEN SO ANGRY IN ME ACTUAL LIFE. ME FELLA BOUGHT ME ENGAGEMENT RING IN POXY DEALZ!!!! THE TICK WENT INTO ARGOS THEN AND BOUGHT HIMSELF AN XBOX! LIKE, IS HE FOR REAL, HUN? ALL ME FAMILY AN' ALL SAY I CAN DO WAY BETTER. I DON'T KNOW WHA' TO DO THOUGH COS WE'RE GOIN' OUT 7 YEARS.

NIKITA: IF I WAS GOIN' OUT WITH SOMEONE FOR 7 YEARS AND THEY GOT ME A RING IN DEALZ, I'D SHOW THEM WHERE THE POXY DOOR IS! GET YIZZERSELF A JAR OF NUTELLA HUN, COS YE DON'T NEED THA' FELLA OF YOURS. HE HAS A LOT OF GROWIN' UP TO DO BY THE SOUNDS OF IT. YOUR MA AN' ALL ARE SPOT ON, A FELLA WHO CHOOSES A GAME CONSOLE OVER HIS FUTURE WIFE IS A PURE SAP. JUST SAYIN' LUV, XOX.

# HOROSCOPES

## ARIES

YE HAVE SOME HEAD ON YE BUT A GOOD HEAD - YE KNOW EXACTLY WHA' YOU'RE LOOKIN' FOR AND YOU'LL DO ANYTHIN' TO GET IT. KEEP GOIN' HUN, FAIR PLAY.

## TAURUS

SOMEONE IS TALKIN' BEHIND YIZZER BACK AND YOU'LL SOON FIND OUT WHO YIZZER REAL FRIENDS ARE. KEEP YIZZER HEAD HELD HIGH AND TELL THEM SAPS 'SEE YA LATER, BYE'.

## GEMINI

YE NEED TO COP ON AND START MINDIN' YIZZERSELF. YE ALWAYS PUT OTHER PEOPLE BEFORE YOU, NOW IT'S TIME TO LOOK OUT FOR THE NO.1 STUN HUN AND TREAT YIZZERSELF.

## CANCER

WOULD YE EVER STOP! THERE'S SOME MAD BAD KARMA COMIN' YIZZER WAY FOR SOMETHIN' YE DONE, SO I'D WATCH ME BACK IF I WAS YOU, HUN. SWEAR. VERY BAD.

## LEO

YOU'RE A DAMP YOKE AND EVERYONE KNOWS IT, BUT SO DO YOU. GET YIZZER HEAD OUT OF YIZZER ARSE AND STOP THINKIN' YOU'RE LIKE BEYONCÉ, YE TICK.

## VIRGO

ME MYSTICAL HUN BUN IS TELLIN' ME THA' YOU'RE PREGGERS, LUV. IF YOU'RE NOT THEN I MUST BE SENSIN' A FOOD BABY, IF I AM THEN YE NEED TO GO TOILET. VERY SORRY 'BOUT THA' LUV, XO.

## LIBRA

IF I WAS YOU I'D BUY A
COUPLE OF SCRATCH CARDS
AND A LOTTO COS A LUCKY
STREAK IS COMIN' YIZZER
WAY. OH! DELIGHTED
FOR YE, HUN. GERRUPPP!!

## SCORPIO

YOU'RE ALWAYS HAVIN' A
MOAN AND YOU'RE STARTIN' TO
WRECK PEOPLE'S HEADS. CALM
DOWN AND RELAX. DO SOME
JUMPIN' JACKS TO GET THA'
BAD MOOD OUT OF YE AND
YOU'LL BE GRAND, NO BOTHER.

## SAGITTARIUS

LOVE IS IN THE AIR, EITHER
THA' OR I CAN SMELL A CHICKEN
FILLET ROLL SOMEWHERE. KEEP
AN EYE OUT COS YOUR PRINCE
IS COMIN' UP THE ROAD ANY
DAY NOW IN HIS HONDA CIVIC.

## CAPRICORN

I SMELL A RAT! IF YOU'VE
BEEN TALKIN' BEHIND YOUR
HUN'S BACK WELL THEN IT'S
DEFO COMIN' FROM YOU. RULE
NUMBER I, YE NEVER RAT ON
YIZZER SQUAD.

## AQUARIUS

YOU'RE ALWAYS UP
FOR A LAUGH AND EVERYONE
LOVES YE. YE BRING GOOD
VIBES TO ANY PARTY AND
IT ISN'T THE SAME WITHOUT
YE. KEEP BEIN' YIZZERSELF.

## PISCES

WOULD YE EVER STOP BEATIN'
YIZZERSELF UP ALL THE TIME.
GIVE YIZZERSELF A BREAK.
PUT THE FEET UP, KETTLE ON
AND WATCH A JEZZA RE-RUN.
YE DESERVE A DAY OFF, HUN.

# PRAYIN' TO SAINT ANTHONY TO FIND YE THE STRENGTH TO DEAL WITH POXES ON A DAILY BASIS

173

# ADIDAS
## ALL DAY
## I DREAM
## ABOUT
### SPICEBAGS

IF YOU'RE HAVIN
FELLA PROBLEMS
I FEEL BAD
FOR YE, HUN
I GOT 99 PROBLEMS
BUT BEIN'
STUNNIN' AIN'T 1

## ★ SOAP ★ DRINKIN' GAME

**RITA!** · CORONATION ST ·

WHA' ELSE WOULD YE BE DOIN' WHEN YOU'RE GETTIN' READY ON A FRIDAY NIGH' AND THERE'S DOUBLE CORRIE ON? SWEAR DOWN! THIS GAME WILL HAVE YE ON A WHOPPER BUZZ HEADIN' INTO TOWN WITH THE HUNS. ALL YE NEED IS YIZZER PRE-DRINKS AND A TELLY, OBVIOUSLY, SO YE CAN WATCH IT.

# THE RULES

- TAKE A SUP EVERYTIME SALLY GOES ON A RANT.
- TAKE TWO SUPS WHEN NORRIS IS HAVIN' A GOSSIP.
- DRINK HALF YIZZER BOTTLE OR CAN WHEN AUDREY SAYS 'HMM'.
- TAKE ANOTHER SUP WHEN SOMEONE WALKS INTO ROY'S.
- ANOTHER SUP IF THEY'RE SERVED UP A MASSIVE FRY.
- DANCE LIKE A MAD YOKE WHENEVER YE SEE KEVIN.
- TAKE A SUP WHEN CILLA SAYS 'MY KIRKY'.
- DOWN YIZZER DRINK WHEN SOMETHIN' GOES WRONG IN THE PLATT HOUSE.
- SHOUT 'GERRRUPP' AND DOWN WHAT'S LEFT IN YOUR GLASS WHEN SOMEONE'S SOBBIN'.
- KNOCK BACK YIZZER DRINK IF SOMEONE DIES.

# SWEAR I HAVEN'T

RIGH', THIS IS LIKE 'NEVER HAVE I EVER' EXCEPT IT'S CALLED 'SWEAR I HAVEN'T'. YE NEED ABOUT 6 PEOPLE TO KEEP THE BALL ROLLIN'. WHA' MAKES IT DIFFERENT IS INSTEAD OF SAYIN' 'NEVER HAVE I EVER' YE SAY 'SWEAR I HAVEN'T' INSTEAD.

## THE RULES

- EVERYONE HAS THEIR OWN DRINK, AT LEAST 3 BOTTLES.
- YE HAVE TO SAY 'SWEAR I HAVEN'T' OUT LOUD AT EVERY TURN.
  IF YE FORGET TO SAY IT THEN YE HAVE TO DOWN YIZZER DRINK.
- IF SOMEONE HAS DRINK LEFT BY THE END OF THE GAME THEN
  THEY LOSE.
- IF YE INTERRUPT SOMEONE'S 'SWEAR I HAVEN'T' YE CAN'T TALK FOR
  2 MINUTES, AND IF YE DO THEN YOU'RE OUT.

AND THAT'S ALL YE NEED TO KNOW TO PLAY. IT'S MAD SIMPLE SO YE CAN EVEN PLAY WHEN YOU'RE IN A HOOP!

# WHAT'S YOUR FELLA'S NAME?

 ♥ ♥

**MONTH YE WERE BORN**

**FIRST LETTER OF YIZZER NAME**

| | |
|---|---|
| JAN | MAD MICKEY |
| FEB | LONG YOKE |
| MAR | BATTERED SAUSAGE |
| APR | SCAREDY FRIDGET |
| MAY | BLUE BALL |
| JUN | HAIRY HOOP |
| JUL | CIDER GULPIN' |
| AUG | SAGGY SACK |
| SEP | TESCO JOHNNY |
| OCT | WET SOCK |
| NOV | TINY TICK |
| DEC | COTTON BOTTOM |

| | | | | |
|---|---|---|---|---|
| A | DZZZOPE | N | CREEP |
| B | RIDE | O | MUNCHER |
| C | SAP | P | SICK STAIN |
| D | ARSE | Q | LASH |
| E | PLEB | R | GOAT |
| F | APE | S | FLAMINGO |
| G | RASHER | T | CRACKER |
| H | SPA | U | MUPPET |
| I | DAZZLER | V | CURRY |
| J | POX | W | CODDLE |
| K | WILLY | X | CRIPS |
| L | RIBBON | Y | VINEGAR |
| M | BISCUIT | Z | LEMON |

# WHAT'S YOUR STUN HUN NAME?

**MONTH YE WERE BORN**

**FIRST LETTER OF YIZZER NAME**

| JAN | STUN |
| FEB | ROTTEN WRECK |
| MAR | WET MESS |
| APR | GAWJUS |
| MAY | LITTLE TICK |
| JUN | SCARLEH |
| JUL | FANNY SPLIT |
| AUG | CURRY FINGER |
| SEP | ACRYLIC LIP |
| OCT | ORANGE LEG |
| NOV | TESCO WINE |
| DEC | MASSO |

| A | DIDDIES |
| B | HOOP |
| C | FANNY |
| D | HUN |
| E | FACE |
| F | FLAPS |
| G | PRINCESS |
| H | SCALP |
| I | SPICEBAG |
| J | CRIPS |
| K | TOILET ROLL |
| L | LASH |
| M | SAP |

| N | DOPE |
| O | BITCH |
| P | YOKE |
| Q | BUN |
| R | TICK |
| S | POX |
| T | BISCUIT |
| U | TAN |
| V | LASHES |
| W | TESCO BAG |
| X | RIM |
| Y | BITS |
| Z | LEGGINS |

# POXY
# DICTIONARY

EVER WONDER WHA' I'M EVEN SAYIN'? NOT FROM THE NORTHSIDE AND DON'T GET SOME OF ME SLANG? SAY NO MORE! NOW YE CAN LEARN SOME OF ME MOST COMMON PHRASES I USE EVERY POXY DAY.

# MASSIVE

SOMETHIN' OR SOMEONE GORGEOUS.

**EXAMPLES**

1. 'OH! THA' YOUNG FELLA IS BLEEDIN' MASSIVE!'

2. 'THA' TOP IS MASSIVE, HUN.'

3. 'YE LOOK MASSIVE, WOULD YE EVER STOP! IMAGE OF KYLIE JENNER.'

# SAP

SOMEONE WHO DOESN'T THINK OR WHO
DOES STUPID OR HARMLESS THINGS.

EXAMPLES

1. 'ANTO, YE FORGOT TO RECORD BIG
   BROTHER, YE SAP.'

2. 'YE BLEEDIN' SAP YE.'

3. 'THA' YOUNG ONE IS A SAP. SHE
   THINKS SHE'S DEADLY BUT SHE'S NOT.'

# HUN

A TERM OF ENDEARMENT AND A
MASSIVE LOOKIN' MOTH FROM DUBLIN.

1. 'AH HEYA HUN, WHAT'S THE STORY?'

2. 'YE LOOK MASSIVE HUN, SWEAR!'

3. 'SHE'S SOME HUN FOR ONE HUN. TELLIN'
   YE, GOK WAN HASN'T A PATCH.'

# GAS

**MEANING**

SOMETHIN' OR SOMEONE
HILARIOUS.

**EXAMPLES**

1. 'AH HE'S BLEEDIN' GAS, WOULD YE
   EVER STOP!'

2. 'THAT'S GAS.'

3. 'ISN'T IT GAS THE WAY I HAD A
   TENNER THERE AND NOW IT'S GONE,
   WHICH ONE OF YIZ TOOK IT?'

# POX

## MEANING

SOMEONE WHO'S MAD ANNOYIN' OR
SOMETHIN' UNBEARABLE.

## EXAMPLES

1. 'ANTO WILL YE LEAVE ME ALONE, YE POX.'

2. 'MEN, THEY'RE ALL THE POXY SAME.'

3. 'THIS IS A LOAD OF POX, ORDERED THA'
   CURRY AN HOUR AGO.'

# TICK

**MEANING**

SOMEONE WHO DOESN'T USE
THEIR NOGGIN'.

**EXAMPLES**

1. 'AWH, YOU'RE A BLEEDIN' TICK SAYIN'
   THA' TO HIM.'

2. 'YOU FOR REAL? YE TICK.'

3. 'THA' YOUNG ONE'S A TICK, SHE
   THOUGHT BABIES CAME FROM
   YOUR BELLYBUTTON UNTIL SHE WAS 16.'

# RIDE

SOMEONE WHO'S REALLY GOOD LOOKIN'.
IT'S ALSO USED INSTEAD OF SEX, AS IN
'TO RIDE' SOMEONE.

**EXAMPLES**

1. 'OH I'D LOVE A GOOD RIDE NOW, HAVEN'T
   HAD ONE IN OVER 6 MONTHS.'

2. 'TOM HARDY IS A BLEEDIN' RIDE.'

3. 'ANTO'S AFTER TEXTIN' ME LOOKIN'
   FOR THE RIDE. I TOLD HIM HOLLYOAKS
   IS ON.'

# HOOP

YOUR ARSE, OR A NICE LOOKIN' ARSE.
YE CAN ALSO USE IT TO DESCRIBE
YOUR HUNGOVER STATE.

**EXAMPLES**

1. 'HOOP ON YOUR ONE.'

2. 'KIM KARDASHIAN HAS SOME HOOP.'

3. 'AWH I'M IN A HOOP, NEVER DRINKIN' AGAIN'.

# STUN HUN

SOMETHIN' OR SOMEONE
WHO LOOKS STUNNIN'.

1. 'THEM LEGGINS ARE STUN HUN.'

2. 'AWH, YE LOOK STUNNIN' HUN.'

3. 'MANDY'S NEW BABY IS A LIL' STUN HUN,
   SHE'S ONLY GORGEOUS.'

# MELT

## MEANING

SOMETHIN' OR SOMEONE WHO WRECKS YOUR
HEAD, BUT IT CAN ALSO MEAN SOMETHIN'
HEART WARMIN' LIKE TO MELT YIZZER HEART.

## EXAMPLES

1. 'ME HEAD'S MELTED DOIN' ALL THIS
   RUNNIN' AROUND, SWEAR.'

2. 'AWH STOP, HE'S A HEAD MELT.'

3. 'AH LOOK AT THA' LIL' GOAT WITH ONE
   LEG HOPPIN' AROUND ON FACEBOOK,
   HE'S A TROOPER. ME HEART'S MELTIN', STOP!'

# LIKE

## MEANING

A WORD THA' I USE ALL THE POXY TIME AND NEVER KNOW WHEN I'M SAYIN' IT, LIKE. HATE WHEN PEOPLE ARE LIKE, 'YE SAID LIKE 20 TIMES'. AND POXY WHA'?

## EXAMPLES

1. 'YE, I LIKE HIM HUN, HE'S ALRIGH' ISN'T HE?'

2. 'IT'S 3 FOR 1 IN DEALZ, LIKE YE KNOW LIKE.'

3. 'SWEAR LIKE, YE WANT TO SEE THA' FELLA WHO WAS IN THE SPAR. IN BITS HE WAS, FALLIN' ALL OVER THE SHOP LIKE.'

# DOPE

A MUPPET, AKA IDIOT - SOMEONE
WHO HAS NO COP ON WHATSOEVER.

**EXAMPLES**

1. 'SHUUP YOU, YE BLEEDIN' DDDZZZOPPPE.'

2. 'YOUR MAN'S A BLEEDIN' DOPE.'

3. 'DON'T MIND HIM HUN, HE DOESN'T
   SEE A GOOD THING WHEN IT'S
   RIGH' IN FRONT OF HIM, THE DDZZOPPE.'

# HACK

## MEANING

SOMETHIN' OR SOMEONE HORRIBLE LOOKIN'
- SOMETHIN' THAT'S PURE ROTTEN!

## EXAMPLES

1. 'THE HACK OF HER, SWEAR.'

2. 'OH THE HACK OF ME, WOULD YE STOP!'

3. 'THE HACK OF THEM RUNNERS, HAD THEM
   3 YEARS AGO.'

# FRIDGET

SOMEONE WHO'S NEVER KISSED SOMEONE
AND USED TONGUES.

EXAMPLES

1. 'YE BIG SCAREDY FRIDGET.'

2. 'ARE YOU A FRIDGET?'

3. 'I'M NOT A FRIDGET, MET SOMEONE ON
   ME HOLIDAYS.'

# MEET

## MEANING

TO KISS SOMEONE USIN' YOUR TONGUE, A
DUBLIN RIGH' OF PASSAGE.

## EXAMPLES

1. 'WILL YE MEET ME MATE?'

2. 'EH NO, SORRY, NOT MEETIN' YOU.'

3. 'TANYA MET SHITEY O'REILLY, CAN'T
   BELIEVE IT!'

# YOKE

SOMEONE WHO'S A GOOD LAUGH - A MAD YOKE.
IT'S ALSO USED TO REPLACE SOMETHIN' YOU'VE
FORGOTTEN THE WORD FOR.

## EXAMPLES

1. 'HE'S A MAD YOKE! BLEEDIN' GAS HE IS.'

2. 'HERE, WILL YE PASS ME OVER THA' YOKE?'

3. 'YE KNOW THA' YOKE, THA' ONE OVER THERE.'

# VERDY GOOD

## MEANING

SOMETHIN' THAT'S VERY GOOD. IT'S ALSO A WAY TO GET SOMEONE TO STOP TALKIN' WHEN YOU'VE NO INTEREST OR NO IDEA WHAT THE POX IS ON ABOUT.

## EXAMPLES

1. 'AH THAT'S VERDY GOOD, BRILLIANT HUN.'

2. 'YE WON THE LOTTO? VERDY GOOD, VERDY GOOD.'

3. 'ME MA JUST BOUGHT A NEW DUVET COVER YESTERDAY.'
   'AH, VERDY GOOD.'

# SNAPPIN'

## MEANING

TO GO ON A MAD ONE. WHEN YOU'RE MAD AGRO
BECAUSE SOMETHIN' HAS GONE WRONG OR HASN'T
GONE YIZZER WAY.

## EXAMPLES

1. 'I'M ONLY SNAPPIN', HUN.'

2. 'I'M SNAPPIN', ME CURRY NEVER ARRIVED.'

3. 'SNAPPIN' I MISSED EASTENDERS.'

# SKETCH

## MEANING

TO RUN FOR YIZZER POXY LIFE. USUALLY
SAID WHEN DOIN' A KNICK-KNACK OR
RUNNIN' FROM THE GARDA.

## EXAMPLES

1. 'SKETCH! MRS FITZ IS IN THE ILAC, I CAN'T
   GET CAUGHT ON THE MITCH AGAIN.'

2. 'SKETCH! THE GARDA.'

3. 'SKETCH! I'M AFTER RINGIN' ANTO'S MA'S
   DOORBELL WHILE CORRIE IS ON.'

# SWEAR

## MEANING

WHEN SOMEONE SAYS 'SWEAR' YE CAN TAKE THEIR WORD THA' IT'S DEFO TRUE, UNLESS THEY'RE A LYIN' POX.

## EXAMPLES

1. 'SWEAR ON ME NANNY'S LIFE I DID.'

2. 'SWEAR ME HEAD'S POXY MELTED.'

3. 'I'LL GO ON A MAD ONE IF THA' TICK FORGOT ME CURRY SAUCE AGAIN, SWEAR.'

# ACKNOWLEDGEMENTS

I'D LIKE TO THANK ME NANNY FIRST OF ALL, FOR MAKIN' ME, LIKE, 1,000 CUPS OF TEA THROUGHOUT THE PROCESS OF MAKIN' THIS STUNNIN' BOOK. SHE'S THE CHICKEN IN A SPICEBAG - BEST NANNY IN THE WORLD.

TO ME FAMILY, ME DA AND ME SISTER ORLA, WHO SUPPORTED ME EVERY STEP OF THE POXY WAY, AND TO THE REST OF ME FAMILY WHO I GOT TO SHARE THIS WHOPPER EXPERIENCE WITH (WON'T SAY WHO ME FAVOURITE AUNTY IS COS I LOVE YIZ ALL THE SAME, RIGH').

TO ME FELLA KARL FOR BEIN' ME ONE AN' ONLY, BEST FELLA IN THE WORLD, STOP! AND TO HIS FAMILY FOR PUTTIN' UP WITH ME TALKIN' ABOUT THIS BOOK EVERY TIME I POXY SEE THEM.

TO EVERYONE ELSE WHO'S SOUND WHO WAS THERE TO SUPPORT ME - YIZ KNOW WHO YE ALL ARE.

TO ALL THE TEAM IN GILL BOOKS. SHOUT OUT TO CATHERINE GOUGH FOR HELPIN' ME WITH ME SPELLINS, BANG ON SO SHE IS, AND JEN PATTON FOR SORTIN' THIS BOOK RIGH' OUT AND MAKIN' SURE IT'S ON FLEEK, SHE'S DEADLY! TO SARAH LIDDY FOR CONTACTIN' ME IN THE FIRST PLACE AND, OF COURSE, ME MAIN MOTH FAITH O' GRADY FOR BEIN' A WHOPPER AGENT, SHE PUTS THE 'SPICE' IN 'SPICEBAG', MAD SOUND.